园 丁 集

· 汉英对照 ·

[印]泰戈尔 著　王钦刚 译

THE

GARDENER

四川文艺出版社

图书在版编目（CIP）数据

园丁集：汉英对照 /（印）泰戈尔著；王钦刚译. — 成都：四川文艺出版社，2023.10

ISBN 978-7-5411-6764-5

Ⅰ.①园… Ⅱ.①泰… ②王… Ⅲ.①诗集 - 印度 - 现代 - 英、汉 Ⅳ.①I351.25

中国国家版本馆CIP数据核字（2023）第171799号

YUAN DING JI （HAN YING DUI ZHAO）

园丁集（汉英对照）

[印]泰戈尔 著

王钦刚 译

出 品 人	谭清洁
责任编辑	张亮亮
封面设计	叶 茂
内文设计	史小燕
责任校对	段 敏
责任印制	崔 娜

出版发行　四川文艺出版社（成都市锦江区三色路238号）
网　　址　www.scwys.com
电　　话　028-86361802（发行部）　　028-86361781（编辑部）

排　　版　四川最近文化传播有限公司
印　　刷　成都东江印务有限公司
成品尺寸　130mm×185mm　　　　开　本　32开
印　　张　8.25　　　　　　　　　字　数　170千
版　　次　2023年10月第一版　　　印　次　2023年10月第一次印刷
书　　号　ISBN 978-7-5411-6764-5
定　　价　49.80元

序

本书中关于爱情和人生的大部分抒情诗，译自孟加拉语，其写作时间比《吉檀迦利》中收录的一系列宗教诗要早得多。

译文并非总是直译——有时节略，有时意译。

罗宾德拉纳特·泰戈尔

PREFACE

Most of the lyrics of love and life, the translations of which from Bengali are published in this book, were written much earlier than the series of religious poems contained in the book named *Gitanjali*.

The translations are not always literal—the originals being sometimes abridged and sometimes paraphrased.

RABINDRANATH TAGORE

目　录

1

臣仆

请垂怜您的臣仆，我的女王！

女王

集会已然结束，我的臣仆们皆已散去。你为何姗姗来迟？

臣仆

您对别人已各有封赏，而今该我粉墨登场。

我来问您还有什么差事，留给您最后一个臣仆。

女王

为时已晚，何必指望？

臣仆

请让我做您花园里的园丁。

女王

荒唐！

臣仆

我将放下其他的事情。

我把我的剑与矛丢弃于尘土之中。不要派我去遥远的宫廷；不要命我开启新的征程。求您让我做您花园里的园丁。

女王

意欲何为？

臣仆

愿为您悠闲的时光效劳。

我要使您清晨漫步的草径保持新鲜，您的双足将步步受到甘心赴死繁花的欢迎礼赞。

我要在七叶树的枝间摇荡您的秋千，傍晚的月亮挣扎着穿过叶间来亲吻您的裙衫。

我要用香油把您床边点燃的灯盏添满，我要用檀香和藏红花膏为您的足凳装饰美妙的图案。

女王

何以为报？

臣仆

请允许我握住您柔荑纤手，把花环套上您的玉腕；请允许我以无忧花瓣的红浆来点染您的脚掌，吻去流连其间的尘埃斑斑。

女王

我的臣仆，我赐你得偿所愿，你将成为园丁，掌管我的花园。

1

Servant

Have mercy upon your servant, my queen!

Queen

The assembly is over and my servants are all gone. Why do you come at this late hour?

Servant

When you have finished with others, that is my time.

I come to ask what remains for your last servant to do.

Queen

What can you expect when it is too late?

Servant

Make me the gardener of your flower garden.

Queen

What folly is this?

Servant

I will give up my other work.

I throw my swords and lances down in the dust. Do not send me to distant courts; do not bid me undertake new conquests. But make me the gardener of your flower garden.

Queen

What will your duties be?

Servant

The service of your idle days.

I will keep fresh the grassy path where you walk in the morning, where your feet will be greeted with praise at every step by the flowers eager for death.

I will swing you in a swing among the branches of the *saptaparna*, where the early evening moon will struggle to kiss your skirt through the leaves.

I will replenish with scented oil the lamp that burns by your bedside, and decorate your footstool with sandal and saffron paste in wondrous designs.

Queen

What will you have for your reward?

Servant

To be allowed to hold your little fists like tender lotus-buds and slip flower chains over your wrists; to tinge the soles of your feet with the red juice of *ashoka* petals and kiss away the speck of dust that may chance to linger there.

Queen

Your prayers are granted, my servant, you will be the gardener of my flower garden.

2

"唉，诗人，夜幕将临，你正华发渐生。

"在孤寂的沉思中，你可听到来生的音信？"

"夜幕降临，"诗人说，"虽然天色已晚，我正在聆听，或许有来自村里呼唤的声音。

"我在眺望，两颗年轻流浪的心是否相逢，两双渴望的眼睛是否在祈求音乐来打破彼此的沉默，为他们诉说衷肠。

"假如我坐在人生的岸上，冥想着来世与死亡，有谁来编织他们热情的诗行？

"傍晚的星辰消隐无踪。

"在寂静的河畔，火葬堆的微光慢慢不见。

"残月朦胧，传来废宅的院中豺狼的嗥叫声声。

"假如有离家的游子来此守夜，低头聆听暗夜的细语呢喃；假如我关上大门，企图摆脱尘世的羁绊，有谁把人生的秘密低语在他的耳畔？

　　"华发渐生，微不足道。

　　"我永远和村子里最年轻的人一样年轻，和最年老的人一样年老。

　　"有的人面露甜蜜而纯朴的微笑，有的人眼含会心的闪耀。

　　"有的人在白天泪如泉涌，有的人在暗夜泣不成声。

　　"他们都需要我，我无暇忧思来生。

　　"我和每个人都同龄，又何惧华发<u>丛生</u>？！"

2

"Ah, poet, the evening draws near; your hair is turning grey.

"Do you in your lonely musing hear the message of the hereafter?"

"It is evening," the poet said, "and I am listening because some one may call from the village, late though it be.

"I watch if young straying hearts meet together, and two pairs of eager eyes beg for music to break their silence and speak for them.

"Who is there to weave their passionate songs, if I sit on the shore of life and contemplate death and the beyond?

"The early evening star disappears.

"The glow of a funeral pyre slowly dies by the silent river.

"Jackals cry in chorus from the courtyard of the deserted

house in the light of the worn-out moon.

"If some wanderer, leaving home, come here to watch the night and with bowed head listen to the murmur of the darkness, who is there to whisper the secrets of life into his ears if I, shutting my doors, should try to free myself from mortal bonds?

"It is a trifle that my hair is turning grey.

"I am ever as young or as old as the youngest and the oldest of this village.

"Some have smiles, sweet and simple, and some a sly twinkle in their eyes.

"Some have tears that well up in the daylight, and others tears that are hidden in the gloom.

"They all have need for me, and I have no time to brood over the afterlife.

"I am of an age with each, what matter if my hair turns grey?"

3

清晨，我向大海里撒网。

我从深渊里拖出的东西奇形怪状、瑰丽异常——有的闪耀如微笑，有的闪亮如泪光，有的羞红如新娘的脸庞。

当我背着一天的收获回到家时，我的爱人正懒洋洋地坐在花园里撕扯着花叶。

我迟疑了片刻，便把拖出来的东西放在她的脚边，默默地站在一旁。

她瞥了一眼，说道："这是些什么奇怪的东西？我不知道它们有什么用处！"

我羞愧地低头思量："我没有为此而奋斗，也没有从市场采购；这些并不适于送给她当作礼物。"

于是我通宵达旦，一件件把它们丢到街上。

清晨，行人来来往往；他们捡起来，把它们带向远方。

3

In the morning I cast my net into the sea.

I dragged up from the dark abyss things of strange aspect and strange beauty—some shone like a smile, some glistened like tears, and some were flushed like the cheeks of a bride.

When with the day's burden I went home, my love was sitting in the garden idly tearing the leaves of a flower.

I hesitated for a moment, and then placed at her feet all that I had dragged up, and stood silent.

She glanced at them and said, "What strange things are these? I know not of what use they are!"

I bowed my head in shame and thought, "I have not fought for these, I did not buy them in the market; they are not fit gifts for her."

Then the whole night through I flung them one by one into the street.

In the morning travellers came; they picked them up and carried them into far countries.

4

唉，他们为什么把我的房子建在通往市镇的路旁？
他们把满载的船只停泊在我的树旁。

他们来来往往，任意游逛。

我坐着，望着，消磨着时光。

我无法把他们赶走。而时光就这样一去不回头。

他们的脚步声昼夜不停地在我门前响动。

"我不认识你们。"我的喊声徒劳无用。

有些人与我携手同行，有些人与我臭味相投，有些人与我血脉相通，有些人与我在梦中相逢。

我无法把他们打发。我招呼他们道："谁愿意来我的房子就来吧。是的，来吧。"

清晨，寺庙鸣钟。

他们提着篮子走来。

他们的双脚玫瑰般红。他们的脸上泛着晨曦的光彩。

我无法把他们打发。我招呼他们道："到我的花园里来采花吧。来这里吧。"

　　正午，大殿门口响起锣声。
　　我不懂他们为何放下营生，而在我篱畔流连忘返。
　　他们发间的花儿苍白而凋零；他们长笛里的音调无力而慵懒。
　　我无法把他们赶走。我招呼他们道："我的树荫下很凉爽。来吧，朋友。"

　　夜里，蟋蟀在林中唧唧而鸣。
　　是谁缓步来到我门前把门轻轻敲动？
　　我朦朦胧胧看见他的脸，却沉默无言，四周尽是寂静的天空。
　　我无法赶走我沉默的宾朋。我透过黑暗望着他的脸，而幻梦的时间流逝无踪。

4

Ah me, why did they build my house by the road to the market town?

They moor their laden boats near my trees.

They come and go and wander at their will.

I sit and watch them; my time wears on.

Turn them away I cannot. And thus my days pass by.

Night and day their steps sound by my door.

Vainly I cry, "I do not know you."

Some of them are known to my fingers, some to my nostrils, the blood in my veins seems to know them, and some are known to my dreams.

Turn them away I cannot. I call them and say, "Come to my house whoever chooses. Yes, come."

In the morning the bell rings in the temple.

They come with their baskets in their hands.

Their feet are rosy red. The early light of dawn is on their faces.

Turn them away I cannot. I call them and I say, "Come to my garden to gather flowers. Come hither."

In the mid-day the gong sounds at the palace gate.

I know not why they leave their work and linger near my hedge.

The flowers in their hair are pale and faded; the notes are languid in their flutes.

Turn them away I cannot. I call them and say, "The shade is cool under my trees. Come, friends."

At night the crickets chirp in the woods.

Who is it that comes slowly to my door and gently knocks?

I vaguely see the face, not a word is spoken, the stillness of the sky is all around.

Turn away my silent guest I cannot. I look at the face through the dark, and hours of dreams pass by.

5

我坐立不安。我渴望的远在天边。

我心不在焉，渴望触摸那幽暗的远方的边缘。

哦，遥远的彼岸！哦，你笛声的热切的呼唤！

我忘了，我总是忘了，我没有飞翔的翅膀，我永远被束缚在这个地方。

我渴望，我无眠，我是一个异客远在异乡。

你的气息扑面而来，低语着一个不可能的希望。

我的心听得懂你的语言，就像懂得自己的一样。

哦，遥不可及的远方！哦，你笛声的热切的呼唤！

我忘了，我总是忘了，我不知路在何方，我没有天马奔向远方。

我无精打采，我是自己心里的流浪汉。

在慵懒时光的日霭中，你浩瀚的幻象在天空的蔚蓝中显现！

哦，海角天边！哦，你笛声的热切的呼唤！

我忘了，我总是忘了，在我独居的地方，到处紧闭着门窗！

5

I am restless. I am athirst for faraway things.

My soul goes out in a longing to touch the skirt of the dim distance.

O Great Beyond, O the keen call of thy flute!

I forget, I ever forget, that I have no wings to fly, that I am bound in this spot evermore.

I am eager and wakeful, I am a stranger in a strange land.

Thy breath comes to me whispering an impossible hope.

Thy tongue is known to my heart as its very own.

O Far-to-seek, O the keen call of thy flute!

I forget, I ever forget, that I know not the way, that I have not the winged horse.

I am listless, I am a wanderer in my heart.

In the sunny haze of the languid hours, what vast vision of

thine takes shape in the blue of the sky!

O Farthest end, O the keen call of thy flute!

I forget, I ever forget, that the gates are shut everywhere
in the house where I dwell alone!

6

驯养之鸟在笼里，自由之鸟在林中。

他们机缘巧合的相逢，这是命运注定。

自由之鸟大呼："亲爱的，让我们飞向林中。"

笼中之鸟低语："来这里吧，让我们都住在笼中。"

自由之鸟问道："在栅栏间，哪有展翅的空间？"

"唉，"笼中之鸟叹道，"在天空里，我真不知道哪里是栖息的家园。"

自由之鸟呼唤："宝贝儿，高唱森林之歌吧。"

笼中之鸟回应："坐在我的身边，我教你学者的语言。"

自由之鸟高喊："不，不! 歌曲永远不能言传。"

笼中之鸟诉说："我不会森林之歌，我真可怜。"

他们的爱因渴望而热烈，而他们却永远不能比翼飞翔。

他们隔栏相望，枉费他们相知的愿望。

"亲爱的，靠近些吧!"他们在向往中振翅高唱。

自由之鸟大呼："做不到呀，我怕这笼子紧闭的门窗。"

笼中之鸟低语："唉，可怜我无力僵死的翅膀。"

6

The tame bird was in a cage, the free bird was in the forest.

They met when the time came, it was a decree of fate.

The free bird cries, "O my love, let us fly to wood."

The cage bird whispers, "Come hither, let us both live in the cage."

Says the free bird, "Among bars, where is there room to spread one's wings?"

"Alas," cries the cage bird, "I should not know where to sit perched in the sky."

The free bird cries, "My darling, sing the songs of the woodlands."

The cage bird says, "Sit by my side, I'll teach you the speech of the learned."

The forest bird cries, "No, ah no! Songs can never be

taught."

The cage bird says, "Alas for me, I know not the songs of the woodlands."

Their love is intense with longing, but they never can fly wing to wing.

Through the bars of the cage they look, and vain is their wish to know each other.

They flutter their wings in yearning, and sing, "Come closer, my love!"

The free bird cries, "It cannot be, I fear the closed doors of the cage."

The cage bird whispers, "Alas, my wings are powerless and dead."

7

哦，妈妈，年轻的王子要从我们家门前经过，——今天早晨我哪有什么心思干活？

教我怎样编我的辫子，告诉我该穿哪件衣裳？

妈妈，你为什么吃惊地把我打量？

我深知他不会抬头瞥一眼我的云窗；我知道转眼间他就要走出我的视线；只有阑珊的笛声呜咽着从远方传到我的耳旁。

可是年轻的王子要从我们家门前经过，我要在这一刻穿上我最好的衣裳。

哦，妈妈，年轻的王子真的从我们家门前经过，他的马车闪耀着朝阳的金光。

我撩开脸上的面纱，扯下颈上的红宝石项链，丢在他经过的路上。

妈妈，你为什么吃惊地把我打量？

我深知他没有捡起我的项链；我知道它被车轮碾压，

零落成尘土中的一点红斑，而没有人知道我的礼物是给谁的以及它的模样。

可是年轻的王子真的从我们家门前经过，而我把胸前的珍宝丢在了他走来的路上。

7

O mother, the young Prince is to pass by our door, — how can I attend to my work this morning?

Show me how to braid up my hair; tell me what garment to put on.

Why do you look at me amazed, mother?

I know well he will not glance up once at my window; I know he will pass out of my sight in the twinkling of an eye; only the vanishing strain of the flute will come sobbing to me from afar.

But the young Prince will pass by our door, and I will put on my best for the moment.

O mother, the young Prince did pass by our door, and the morning sun flashed from his chariot.

I swept aside the veil from my face, I tore the ruby chain from my neck and flung it in his path.

Why do you look at me amazed, mother?

I know well he did not pick up my chain; I know it was crushed under his wheels leaving a red stain upon the dust, and no one knows what my gift was nor to whom.

But the young Prince did pass by our door, and I flung the jewel from my breast before his path.

8

当我床边的灯熄灭了，我和早起的鸟儿一起醒来。

我坐在打开的窗前，在蓬松的发间戴上新鲜的花环。

在玫瑰色的晨雾中，年轻的旅人沿着大路走来。

他项上戴着珠链，阳光洒在他的花冠上。他停在我的门前，用急切的呼喊问我："她在何方？"

我害羞得无法对他讲："她就是我，年轻的旅人，我就是那个姑娘。"

傍晚来临，华灯未上。

我编着发辫，无精打采。

在落日的余晖中，年轻的旅人驾着马车赶来。

他的马儿嘴里喷着白沫，尘土沾满了他的衣裳。

他在我的门前下车，用疲惫的声音问道："她在何方？"

我害羞得无法对他讲："她就是我，疲惫的旅人，我就是那个姑娘。"

一个四月的晚上。我的屋里灯光明亮。

南风轻柔地吹来。聒噪的鹦鹉在笼里睡梦酣畅。

我的胸衣蔚蓝如同孔雀的颈项，我的披风青翠如同嫩草一样。

我坐在窗前的地上，凝望着空寂无人的街巷。

黑夜漫漫，我不停地哼唱："她就是我，绝望的旅人，我就是那个姑娘。"

8

When the lamp went out by my bed I woke up with the early birds.

I sat at my open window with a fresh wreath on my loose hair.

The young traveller came along the road in the rosy mist of the morning.

A pearl chain was on his neck, and the sun's rays fell on his crown. He stopped before my door and asked me with an eager cry, "Where is she?"

For very shame I could not say, "She is I, young traveller, she is I."

It was dusk and the lamp was not lit.

I was listlessly braiding my hair.

The young traveller came on his chariot in the glow of the setting sun.

His horses were foaming at the mouth, and there was dust on his garment.

He alighted at my door and asked in a tired voice, "Where is she?"

For very shame I could not say, "She is I, young traveller, she is I."

It is an April night. The lamp is burning in my room.

The breeze of the south comes gently. The noisy parrot sleeps in its cage.

My bodice is of the colour of the peacock's throat, and my mantle is green as young grass.

I sit upon the floor at the window watching the deserted street.

Through the dark night I keep humming, "She is I, despairing traveller, she is I."

9

当我在夜里独赴幽会之时，鸟儿不唱，风儿不响，房子静静地站在街道的两旁。

我自己的脚镯却一步一响，使我羞愧难当。

当我在阳台上聆听他脚步的声响，树叶不动，河水仿佛酣睡中哨兵膝上的刀剑一样寂静无声。

是我自己的心在狂野地跳动——我不知道怎样使它平静。

当我的爱人来了，坐在我的身旁，当我的身体颤抖、眼帘低垂的时候，夜色苍茫，风儿吹灭了残缸，云儿把繁星的面纱遮上。

是我自己胸前的珍宝在闪烁发光。我不知道如何将它隐藏。

9

When I go alone at night to my love-tryst, birds do not sing, the wind does not stir, the houses on both sides of the street stand silent.

It is my own anklets that grow loud at every step and I am ashamed.

When I sit on my balcony and listen for his footsteps, leaves do not rustle on the trees, and the water is still in the river like the sword on the knees of a sentry fallen sleep.

It is my own heart that beats wildly—I do not know how to quiet it.

When my love comes and sits by my side, when my body trembles and my eyelids droop, the night darkens, the wind blows out the lamp, and the clouds draw veils over the stars.

It is the jewel at my own breast that shines and gives light. I do not know how to hide it.

10

別忙了，新娘。听，客人来了。

你可听见，他正在轻轻地把门闩摇晃？

留神别让你的脚镯弄出声响，你迎接他的脚步也别过于匆忙。

别忙了，新娘，客人在夜色中来了。

不，这不是阴风，新娘，不要惊慌。

这是四月之望，庭中树影暗淡，头顶天空明亮。

把面纱遮在脸上吧，如果你一定要这样；如果你害怕，就提着灯去门口吧。

不，这不是阴风，新娘，不要惊慌。

如果你害羞，就不必和他说话；你迎接他时，就站在门边吧。

如果他问你话，如果你愿意，你就以沉默低眸作答。

当你掌灯引他进门时，别让你的手镯叮当作响。

如果你害羞，就不必和他说话。

你还没忙完吗，新娘？听，客人来了。
你还没把牛棚里的灯点亮？
你还没把晚祷的供筐准备停当？
你还没在发间点上朱砂象征吉祥？你还没有理过晚妆？
新娘呵，你可听见，客人已经来了？
别忙了。

Let your work be, bride. Listen, the guest has come.

Do you hear, he is gently shaking the chain which fastens the door?

See that your anklets make no loud noise, and that your step is not over-hurried at meeting him.

Let your work be, bride, the guest has come in the evening.

No, it is not the ghostly wind, bride, do not be frightened.

It is the full moon on a night of April; shadows are pale in the courtyard; the sky overhead is bright.

Draw your veil over your face if you must, carry the lamp to the door if you fear.

No, it is not the ghostly wind, bride, do not be frightened.

Have no word with him if you are shy; stand aside by the

door when you meet him.

If he asks you questions, and if you wish to, you can lower your eyes in silence.

Do not let your bracelets jingle when, lamp in hand, you lead him in.

Have no word with him if you are shy.

Have you not finished your work yet, bride? Listen, the guest has come.

Have you not lit the lamp in the cowshed?

Have you not got ready the offering basket for the evening service?

Have you not put the red lucky mark at the parting of your hair, and done your toilet for the night?

O bride, do you hear, the guest has come?

Let your work be!

11

来吧，就这样素面朝天；不要在梳妆上消磨时间。

即使你的辫发松散，即使没有笔直的发缝，即使你胸衣的丝带没有系紧，都不要心心念念。

来吧，就这样素面朝天；不要在梳妆上消磨时间。

来吧，穿越草坪，脚步匆匆。

即使露水把你的脚打湿染成赭红，即使你脚镯上的铃铛摇摇晃晃，即使你项链上的珠子滑落无踪，都不要念念不忘。

来吧，穿越草坪，脚步匆匆。

你可看见云霭遮蔽着苍穹？

鹤群从远远的河岸飞升，荒原上吹过阵阵狂风。

惊牛奔向村里的牛棚。

你可看见云霭遮蔽着苍穹？

你徒然点亮梳妆的灯——它摇曳着熄灭在风中。

谁能看出你的眼睫上没有涂上黛烟？因为比雨云还黑亮的是你的眼睛！

你徒然点亮梳妆的灯——它熄灭在风中。

来吧，就这样素面朝天；不要在梳妆上消磨时间。

谁会在意尚未编就的花环，且不去管尚未扣好的手链。

空中阴云密布——天色已晚。

来吧，就这样素面朝天；不要在梳妆上消磨时间。

11

Come as you are; do not loiter over your toilet.

If your braided hair has loosened, if the parting of your hair be not straight, if the ribbons of your bodice be not fastened, do not mind.

Come as you are; do not loiter over your toilet.

Come, with quick steps over the grass.

If the raddle come from your feet because of the dew, if the rings of bells upon your feet slacken, if pearls drop out of your chain, do not mind.

Come, with quick steps over the grass.

Do you see the clouds wrapping the sky?

Flocks of cranes fly up from the further river-bank and fitful gusts of wind rush over the heath.

The anxious cattle run to their stalls in the village.

Do you see the clouds wrapping the sky?

In vain you light your toilet lamp—it flickers and goes out in the wind.

Who can know that your eyelids have not been touched with lamp-black? For your eyes are darker than rain-clouds.

In vain you light your toilet lamp—it goes out.

Come as you are; do not loiter over your toilet.

If the wreath is not woven, who cares; if the wrist-chain has not been linked, let it be.

The sky is overcast with clouds—it is late.

Come as you are; do not loiter over your toilet.

12

如果你要忙着装满你的水罐，来吧，哦，来我的湖畔。

湖水将环绕着你的脚边，倾诉着秘密，细语呢喃。

欲来的雨，影子落在沙滩；云霭低垂在丛林的蓝色边缘，如你眉上的云鬟。

我深谙你脚步的韵律，仿佛敲打在我的心间。

来吧，哦，来我的湖畔，如果你要装满你的水罐。

如果你想闲坐而慵懒，让你的水罐漂在水面，来吧，哦，来我的湖畔。

草坡青青，野花繁盛。

你的思想如离巢的鸟儿，将飞出你乌溜溜的眼睛。

你的面纱将滑落到你的脚边。

来吧，如果你要闲坐，哦，来我的湖畔。

如果你想停止游戏并跳入水中，来吧，哦，来我的湖畔。

把你蓝色的披风放在湖岸；碧波荡漾，把你拥抱，把你隐藏。

水波不兴，将悄悄吻上你的秀颈，低语在你的耳边。

来吧，如果你想跳入水中，哦，来我的湖畔。

如果你要疯癫，纵身跃入死海，来吧，哦，来我的湖畔。

湖水清凉，深不可言。

湖水暗如无梦的酣眠。

在湖水深处，昼夜难辨，而歌声就是沉默无言。

来吧，如果你想跃入死海，哦，来我的湖畔。

If you would be busy and fill your pitcher, come, O come to my lake.

The water will cling round your feet and babble its secret.

The shadow of the coming rain is on the sands, and the clouds hang low upon the blue lines of the trees like the heavy hair above your eyebrows.

I know well the rhythm of your steps, they are beating in my heart.

Come, O come to my lake, if you must fill your pitcher.

If you would be idle and sit listless and let your pitcher float on the water, come, O come to my lake.

The grassy slope is green, and the wild flowers beyond number.

Your thoughts will stray out of your dark eyes like birds from their nests.

Your veil will drop to your feet.

Come, O come to my lake if you must sit idle.

If you would leave off your play and dive in the water, come, O come to my lake.

Let your blue mantle lie on the shore; the blue water will cover you and hide you.

The waves will stand a-tiptoe to kiss your neck and whisper in your ears.

Come, O come to my lake, if you would dive in the water.

If you must be mad and leap to your death, come, O come to my lake.

It is cool and fathomlessly deep.

It is dark like a sleep that is dreamless.

There in its depths nights and days are one, and songs are silence.

Come, O come to my lake, if you would plunge to your death.

13

我一无所求，只站在林边树后。

黎明的眼睛倦意依旧，露水在空气里残留。

地面上薄雾缭绕，弥漫着湿草慵懒的味道。

你在榕树下挤着牛奶，用你柔嫩的凝脂般的双手。

而我兀立不动。

我默不作声。歌唱的鸟儿躲在丛林之中。

杧果树的花朵飘洒在乡野的小径，引来一只只蜜蜂嘤嘤嗡嗡。

池边湿婆神庙的大门打开，朝拜者开始诵经。

你在挤着牛奶，罐子放在腿上。

我兀立，罐里空空。

我没有走近你的身旁。

庙里锣声响起，此时天光大亮。

驱走的牛群奋蹄而奔，路上尘土飞扬。

女人们从河畔归来，抱着的水罐汩汩作响。

你的手镯叮当，乳沫溢到罐沿上。

晨光渐逝，而我没有走近你的身旁。

13

I asked nothing, only stood at the edge of the wood behind the tree.

Languor was still upon the eyes of the dawn, and the dew in the air.

The lazy smell of the damp grass hung in the thin mist above the earth.

Under the banyan tree you were milking the cow with your hands, tender and fresh as butter.

And I was standing still.

I did not say a word. It was the bird that sang unseen from the thicket.

The mango tree was shedding its flowers upon the village road, and the bees came humming one by one.

On the side of the pond the gate of *Shiva's* temple was opened and the worshipper had begun his chants.

With the vessel on your lap you were milking the cow.

I stood with my empty can.

I did not come near you.

The sky woke with the sound of the gong at the temple.

The dust was raised in the road from the hoofs of the driven cattle.

With the gurgling pitchers at their hips, women came from the river.

Your bracelets were jingling, and foam brimming over the jar.

The morning wore on and I did not come near you.

14

天已过午，竹枝在风中簌簌，不知为何，我在路旁踟蹰。

横斜的树影伸出手臂，挽住流光匆匆的脚步。

噪鹊唱厌了它们的歌曲。

不知为何，我在路旁踟蹰。

低垂的树荫遮住水边的茅屋。

有人在忙着工作，她的手镯在角落里奏乐。

我兀立在茅屋前，不知为何。

片片芥菜地和层层柠果林间，有蜿蜒的小径穿过。

村里的庙宇和渡口的集市前，有蜿蜒的小径穿过。

我停留在茅屋前，不知为何。

那是多年以前清风徐来的三月，春风慵懒细语，柠果花瓣零落于尘土。

水波荡漾，涟漪舐吻着渡口阶沿上的铜壶。
我想起那清风徐来的三月，不知为何。

夜影渐深，牛群归栏。
孤寂的牧场暮色苍茫，村民在河边等候渡船。
我缓步归去，不知为何。

14

I was walking by the road, I do not know why, when the noonday was past and bamboo branches rustled in the wind.

The prone shadows with their outstretched arms clung to the feet of the hurrying light.

The *koels* were weary of their songs.

I was walking by the road, I do not know why.

The hut by the side of the water is shaded by an overhanging tree.

Some one was busy with her work, and her bangles made music in the corner.

I stood before this hut, I know not why.

The narrow winding road crosses many a mustard field, and many a mango forest.

It passes by the temple of the village and the market at the river landing-place.

I stopped by this hut, I do not know why.

Years ago it was a day of breezy March when the murmur of the spring was languorous, and mango blossoms were dropping on the dust.

The rippling water leapt and licked the brass vessel that stood on the landing-step.

I think of that day of breezy March, I do not know why.

Shadows are deepening and cattle returning to their folds.

The light is grey upon the lonely meadows, and the villagers are waiting for the ferry at the bank.

I slowly return upon my steps, I do not know why.

15

我像一只在林荫中飞奔的香獐，为自己的香气疯狂。
风是南风徐来，夜是五月之望。
我迷路，我彷徨，我觅我不可得，我得我不曾想。

从心里走出来翩翩起舞的，是我自己欲望的形象。
闪烁的幻象，翩跹地飞翔。
我想紧紧把它握住，它躲开又把我引入歧途。
我觅我不可得，我得我不曾想。

15

I run as a musk-deer runs in the shadow of the forest mad with his own perfume.

The night is the night of mid-May, the breeze is the breeze of the south.

I lose my way and I wander, I seek what I cannot get, I get what I do not seek.

From my heart comes out and dances the image of my own desire.

The gleaming vision flits on.

I try to clasp it firmly, it eludes me and leads me astray.

I seek what I cannot get, I get what I do not seek.

16

素手相牵，眼波流连：这样开启了我们心的诗篇。

这是三月的月明之夜，空气中凤仙花的芬芳弥漫；我的长笛抛在地上，还有你未编成的花环。

你我之间的爱，如歌一样简单。

你橘黄色的面纱，令我醉眼陶然。

你为我编织的素馨花环，是令我心醉神迷的礼赞。

这个游戏，欲迎还拒、若隐若现；些许娇羞，些许嫣然，还有些甜蜜而徒劳的抵拦。

你我之间的爱，如歌一样简单。

没有超越现实的神秘，没有强求的勉为其难，没有妩媚背后的阴影，没有幽暗深处的窥探。

你我之间的爱，如歌一样简单。

我们不必抛弃一切言语而误入永远沉默的歧途；我们

不必伸手向虚空要求超乎希望的事物。

我们付出，我们获取，都已足够。

我们不曾耽于享乐而从中榨取痛苦的醇酒。

你我之间的爱，如歌一样简单。

Hands cling to hands and eyes linger on eyes: thus begins the record of our hearts.

It is the moonlit night of March; the sweet smell of *henna* is in the air; my flute lies on the earth neglected and your garland of flowers is unfinished.

This love between you and me is simple as a song.

Your veil of the saffron colour makes my eyes drunk.

The jasmine wreath that you wove me thrills to my heart like praise.

It is a game of giving and withholding, revealing and screening again; some smiles and some little shyness, and some sweet useless struggles.

This love between you and me is simple as a song.

No mystery beyond the present; no striving for the

impossible; no shadow behind the charm; no groping in the depth of the dark.

This love between you and me is simple as a song.

We do not stray out of all words into the ever silent; we do not raise our hands to the void for things beyond hope.

It is enough what we give and we get.

We have not crushed the joy to the utmost to wring from it the wine of pain.

This love between you and me is simple as a song.

17

黄鹂在树上歌唱，令我心花怒放。

我们俩住在同一个村庄，那就是我们的一份欢畅。

她心爱的一对羔羊，来我园中的树荫下徜徉。

羔羊若是闯进了我们的麦田，我会把它们抱在臂弯。

我们的村子名叫康姆纳，人们把我们的小河叫安姆纳。

我的名字全村都知道，她的名字叫兰姆娜。

我们之间只隔着一块地。

在我们园里筑巢的蜜蜂，飞到她们那里去采蜜。

她们渡口的落花，顺流漂到我们沐浴的地方。

一筐筐的干草花，从她们的地里来到我们的集市上。

我们的村子名叫康姆纳，人们把我们的小河叫安姆纳。

我的名字全村都知道，她的名字叫兰姆娜。

蜿蜒至她家门口的小巷，春天里弥漫着杧果花的芬芳。

当她们地里的亚麻籽丰收在望，我们地里的大麻正在绽放。

    在她们茅屋上微笑的繁星，送给我们以同样的闪亮。

    雨水涨满了她们的池塘，也令我们的迦昙波树林欢畅。

    我们的村子名叫康旃纳，人们把我们的小河叫安旃纳。

    我的名字全村都知道，她的名字叫兰旃娜。

17

The yellow bird sings in their tree and makes my heart dance with gladness.

We both live in the same village, and that is our one piece of joy.

Her pair of pet lambs come to graze in the shade of our garden trees.

If they stray into our barley field, I take them up in my arms.

The name of our village is *Khanjanā*, and *Anjanā* they call our river.

My name is known to all the village, and her name is *Ranjanā*.

Only one field lies between us.

Bees that have hived in our grove go to seek honey in theirs.

Flowers launched from their landing-stairs come floating by the stream where we bathe.

Baskets of dried *kusm* flowers come from their fields to our market.

The name of our village is *Khanjanā*, and *Anjanā* they call our river.

My name is known to all the village, and her name is *Ranjanā*.

The lane that winds to their house is fragrant in the spring with mango flowers.

When their linseed is ripe for harvest the hemp is in bloom in our field.

The stars that smile on their cottage send us the same twinkling look.

The rain that floods their tank makes glad our *kadam* forest.

The name of our village is *Khanjanā*, and *Anjanā* they call our river.

My name is known to all the village, and her name is *Ranjanā*.

18

当姐妹俩去汲水时，她们来到这个地方便莞尔一笑。

她们一定察觉到，每逢她们去汲水时，总有人站在树后张望。

姐妹俩窃窃私语，当她们经过这个地方。

她们一定猜到了那个人的秘密，每逢她们去汲水时，那个人总站在树后张望。

她们的水罐突然倾倒，水流满地，当她们抵达这个地方。

她们一定发觉到那个人的心在狂跳，每逢她们去汲水时，那个人总站在树后张望。

姐妹俩相视而笑，当她们来到这个地方。

她们轻盈的步伐里带着欢笑，令他魂牵梦绕；每逢她们去汲水时，那个人总站在树后张望。

18

When the two sisters go to fetch water, they come to this spot and they smile.

They must be aware of somebody who stands behind the trees whenever they go to fetch water.

The two sisters whisper to each other when they pass this spot.

They must have guessed the secret of that somebody who stands behind the trees whenever they go to fetch water.

Their pitchers lurch suddenly, and water spills when they reach this spot.

They must have found out that somebody's heart is beating who stands behind the trees whenever they go to fetch water.

The two sisters glance at each other when they come to this spot, and they smile.

There is a laughter in their swift-stepping feet, which makes confusion in somebody's mind who stands behind the trees whenever they go to fetch water.

19

腰间搂着装满的水罐，你从河畔的小径走过。

你为何飞快地回眸，透过飘扬的面纱偷偷地看我？

黑暗里投来的惊鸿一瞥，如一缕清风拂过粼粼的水波，吹向幽暗的水岸。

那惊鸿一瞥，像夜莺穿过昏暗的房间，从洞开的窗户此进彼出，在黑夜里消失不见。

你像藏在山后的星辰，而我是路上的一个过客。

可是当你腰间搂着装满的水罐，从河畔的小径走过，你为何驻足片刻，透过面纱偷偷地看我？

19

You walked by the riverside path with the full pitcher upon your hip.

Why did you swiftly turn your face and peep at me through your fluttering veil?

That gleaming look from the dark came upon me like a breeze that sends a shiver through the rippling water and sweeps away to the shadowy shore.

It came to me like the bird of the evening that hurriedly flies across the lampless room from the one open window to the other, and disappears in the night.

You are hidden as a star behind the hills, and I am a passer-by upon the road.

But why did you stop for a moment and glance at my face through your veil while you walked by the riverside path with the full pitcher upon your hip?

20

日复一日，他来了又走。

去吧，从我的鬓间摘一朵花送给他，我的朋友。

假如他问是谁送的花，求你不要把我的名字告诉他——因为他不过是来了又走。

他席地而坐在树下。

用繁花嫩叶为他铺一个座位吧，我的朋友。

他忧郁的眼神，把忧郁带来我的心头。

他满腹心事，却没有说出口；他只是来了又走。

20

Day after day he comes and goes away.

Go, and give him a flower from my hair, my friend.

If he asks who was it that sent it, I entreat you do not tell him my name—for he only comes and goes away.

He sits on the dust under the tree.

Spread there a seat with flowers and leaves, my friend.

His eyes are sad, and they bring sadness to my heart.

He does not speak what he has in mind; he only comes and goes away.

21

当天色微亮，为何这年轻的游子偏要在我的门前游荡？

当我每次进出经过他的身旁，他的脸庞总吸引着我的目光。

我不知道我该开口还是沉默。为何他偏要在我的门前游荡？

七月的暗夜暗淡无光；秋日的天空碧蓝如洗；南风徐来，令人春心摇荡。

他总是用新鲜的曲调来吟唱。

我放下工作，满眼迷茫。为何他偏要在我的门前游荡？

21

Why did he choose to come to my door, the wandering youth, when the day dawned?

As I come in and out I pass by him every time, and my eyes are caught by his face.

I know not if I should speak to him or keep silent. Why did he choose to come to my door?

The cloudy nights in July are dark; the sky is soft blue in the autumn; the spring days are restless with the south wind.

He weaves his songs with fresh tunes every time.

I turn from my work and my eyes fill with the mist. Why did he choose to come to my door?

22

她的裙边碰到了我，当她匆匆走过我的身旁。

一缕突如其来的春天的馨香，来自一颗心未知的地方。

那怦然心动的触碰转瞬不见，仿佛撕碎的花瓣在微风中飘荡。

它像她身体的叹息和心灵的呢喃，落在我的心上。

22

When she passed by me with quick steps, the end of her skirt touched me.

From the unknown island of a heart came a sudden warm breath of spring.

A flutter of a flitting touch brushed me and vanished in a moment, like a torn flower petal blown in the breeze.

It fell upon my heart like a sigh of her body and whisper of her heart.

23

你为何悠闲地坐在那里，把手镯摆弄得叮当作响？
灌满你的水罐吧。是时候该回家了。

你为何悠闲地拨弄着水花，不时地向路上把某人张望？
灌满你的水罐回家吧。

晨光消逝——幽暗的河水奔流不息。
波浪悠闲地相互低语嬉戏。

流云聚集在远野高地的天边。
它们悠闲地看着你的脸，微笑，流连。
灌满你的水罐回家吧。

23

Why do you sit there and jingle your bracelets in mere idle sport?

Fill your pitcher. It is time for you to come home.

Why do you stir the water with your hands and fitfully glance at the road for some one in mere idle sport?

Fill your pitcher and come home.

The morning hours pass by—the dark water flows on.

The waves are laughing and whispering to each other in mere idle sport.

The wandering clouds have gathered at the edge of the sky on yonder rise of the land.

They linger and look at your face and smile in mere idle sport.

Fill your pitcher and come home.

24

我的朋友，别把你心里的秘密藏起！

悄悄地告诉我，只对我一个人诉说。

你巧笑嫣然，细语呢喃；不是我的耳朵，是我的心倾听着你的语言。

夜色沉沉，庭院深深，鸟巢笼罩着睡意。

告诉我吧，你心里的秘密！从迟疑的泪光里，从沉吟的笑容里，从甜蜜的羞涩和痛苦里。

24

Do not keep to yourself the secret of your heart, my friend!

Say it to me, only to me, in secret.

You who smile so gently, softly whisper, my heart will hear it, not my ears.

The night is deep, the house is silent, the birds' nests are shrouded with sleep.

Speak to me through hesitating tears, through faltering smile, through sweet shame and pain, the secret of your heart!

25

"年轻人，来我们这里吧，老实告诉我们，为何你眼中透着疯狂？"

"我不知喝了什么野生罂粟酒，使我的眼中透着疯狂。"

"唉，好羞!"

"哦，有的人聪明，有的人愚蠢；有的人小心谨慎，有的人漫不经心。有的人眉花眼笑，有的人热泪盈眶——而我的眼中透着疯狂。"

"年轻人，为何你在树荫下伫立良久？"

"我心中的重担使我步履维艰，我就在树荫下伫立良久。"

"唉，好羞!"

"哦，有的人大步向前，有的人踟蹰流连；有的人自由自在，有的人裹足不前——而我心中的重担使我步履维艰。"

25

"Come to us, youth, tell us truly why there is madness in your eyes?"

"I know not what wine of wild poppy I have drunk, that there is this madness in my eyes."

"Ah, shame!"

"Well, some are wise and some foolish, some are watchful and some careless. There are eyes that smile and eyes that weep—and madness is in my eyes."

"Youth, why do you stand so still under the shadow of the tree?"

"My feet are languid with the burden of my heart, and I stand still in the shadow."

"Ah, shame!"

"Well, some march on their way and some linger, some are free and some are fettered—and my feet are languid with the burden of my heart."

26

"你慷慨相赠，我欣然接受。我别无他求。"

"行了，行了，谦逊的乞者，我懂你，你要的是人家拥有的一切。"

"若是给我一朵飘零的落花，我便把它戴在心间。"

"若是花上有刺呢？"

"我便忍受这熬煎。"

"行了，行了，谦逊的乞者，我懂你，你要的是人家拥有的一切。"

"哪怕你只向我投来一瞥爱怜，也将令我至死犹甜。"

"若只是残忍的一瞥呢？"

"我便让它刺穿我的心田。"

"行了，行了，谦逊的乞者，我懂你，你要的是人家拥有的一切。"

26

"What comes from your willing hands I take. I beg for nothing more."

"Yes, yes, I know you, modest mendicant, you ask for all that one has."

"If there be a stray flower for me I will wear it in my heart."

"But if there be thorns?"

"I will endure them."

"Yes, yes, I know you, modest mendicant, you ask for all that one has."

"If but once you should raise your loving eyes to my face it would make my life sweet beyond death."

"But if there be only cruel glances?"

"I will keep them piercing my heart."

"Yes, yes, I know you, modest mendicant, you ask for all that one has."

27

"相信爱，即使它给你带来忧伤。别把你的心扉关
上。"

"呵，不，朋友，你的话晦涩难懂。"

"亲爱的，此心只为悲喜交集的奉献。"

"呵，不，朋友，你的话晦涩难懂。"

"欢娱如露而易逝，忧伤似海而悠长。让忧伤的爱，
在你的眼中醒来。"

"呵，不，朋友，你的话晦涩难懂。"

"阳光灿烂，荷花绽放，随即凋亡。严冬漫漫，它将
不再含苞待放。"

"呵，不，朋友，你的话晦涩难懂。"

27

"Trust love even if it brings sorrow. Do not close up your heart."

"Ah no, my friend, your words are dark, I cannot understand them."

"The heart is only for giving away with a tear and a song, my love."

"Ah no, my friend, your words are dark, I cannot understand them."

"Pleasure is frail like a dewdrop, while it laughs it dies. But sorrow is strong and abiding. Let sorrowful love wake in your eyes."

"Ah no, my friend, your words are dark, I cannot understand them."

"The lotus blooms in the sight of the sun, and loses all that it has. It would not remain in bud in the eternal winter mist."

"Ah no, my friend, your words are dark, I cannot understand them."

28

你疑惑的目光充满悲伤。它渴望了解我的意图，正如月亮想了解大海的真相。

我在你面前自始至终透明敞亮，毫无保留和隐藏。因此你把我当成陌生人一样。

它若是一颗宝石，我便把它锤炼为千百碎片，串成珠链戴在你的颈上。

它若是一朵鲜花，丰满、小巧而芬芳，我便从枝上采下，戴在你的发上。

可它是一颗心，我的心上人。哪里是它的天涯海角？

你不知道这个王国的边界，而你仍是它的女王。

它若只是片刻欢畅，它将巧笑如花绽放，而你便能瞬间看见和领悟。

它若只是些许痛苦，它将化为晶莹的泪行，写出内心深处的秘密，虽然只字未吐。

可它是爱呵，我的心上人。

它有无限的欢乐和痛苦，无穷的渴望和财富。

它和你如同生命一样亲近，却永远像个不完全了解的陌生人。

28

Your questioning eyes are sad. They seek to know my meaning as the moon would fathom the sea.

I have bared my life before your eyes from end to end, with nothing hidden or held back. That is why you know me not.

If it were only a gem, I could break it into a hundred pieces and string them into a chain to put on your neck.

If it were only a flower, round and small and sweet, I could pluck it from its stem to set it in your hair.

But it is a heart, my beloved. Where are its shores and its bottom?

You know not the limits of this kingdom, still you are its queen.

If it were only a moment of pleasure it would flower in an easy smile, and you could see it and read it in a moment.

If it were merely a pain it would melt in limpid tears,

reflecting its inmost secret without a word.

But it is love, my beloved.

Its pleasure and pain are boundless, and endless its wants and wealth.

It is as near to you as your life, but you can never wholly know it.

亲爱的，请对我说！把你所唱的，用言语告诉我。

夜色沉沉。群星在云间消隐。风在树叶间唏嘘。

我要把头发披散。我的蓝色披风像黑夜一样把我抱紧。我要把你的头抱在胸前；在甜蜜的孤寂里，在你的心间细语呢喃。我将闭目倾听。我不会端详你的脸。

当你细语不闻，我们便静坐无言。只有树木在黑暗中低吟。

夜色阑珊。曙光将现。我们将凝眸相顾，然后踏上不同的旅途。

亲爱的，请对我说！把你所唱的，用言语告诉我。

29

Speak to me, my love! Tell me in words what you sang.

The night is dark. The stars are lost in clouds. The wind is sighing through the leaves.

I will let loose my hair. My blue cloak will cling round me like night. I will clasp your head to my bosom; and there in the sweet loneliness murmur on your heart. I will shut my eyes and listen. I will not look in your face.

When your words are ended, we will sit still and silent. Only the trees will whisper in the dark.

The night will pale. The day will dawn. We shall look at each other's eyes and go on our different paths.

Speak to me, my love! Tell me in words what you sang.

30

你是我梦里天空飘着的晚霞。

我永远用爱的渴望来把你描画。

你属于我，属于我。我无尽梦里的居住者！

你的双足因我心头的渴望之光而红艳。我落日之歌的采集者！

你的双唇因我痛苦之酒味而苦中带甜。

你属于我，属于我。我孤寂梦里的居住者！

我用热情的阴影，染黑了你的眼睛。我魂牵梦萦的意中人！

亲爱的，在我音乐的罗网中，我把你俘获，把你抱紧。

你属于我，属于我。我永恒梦里的居住者！

30

You are the evening cloud floating in the sky of my dreams.

I paint you and fashion you ever with my love longings.

You are my own, my own, Dweller in my endless dreams!

Your feet are rosy-red with the glow of my heart's desire, Gleaner of my sunset songs!

Your lips are bitter-sweet with the taste of my wine of pain.

You are my own, my own, Dweller in my lonesome dreams!

With the shadow of my passion have I darkened your eyes, Haunter of the depth of my gaze!

I have caught you and wrapt you, my love, in the net of my music.

You are my own, my own, Dweller in my deathless dreams!

31

我的心是荒野的鸟，在你的眼中找到了天空。

你的眼睛是清晨的摇篮，是繁星的家园。

我的歌迷失在你眼睛的深渊。

且让我翱翔在那片孤寂天空的无限空间。

且让我穿越云层，展翅飞翔在它的阳光中。

31

My heart, the bird of the wilderness, has found its sky in your eyes.

They are the cradle of the morning, they are the kingdom of the stars.

My songs are lost in their depths.

Let me but soar in that sky, in its lonely immensity.

Let me but cleave its clouds and spread wings in its sunshine.

32

亲爱的，告诉我，这一切可是真的？这可是真的？

当我的双眼电光闪现，你胸中的乌云便报之以风雨雷电？

我的双唇真的像初恋绽放的花蕾般香甜？

消逝的五月的回忆还在我的手足间流连？

大地真的因我双足的踏触而震颤？像竖琴弹奏出爱的诗篇？

那么真的是黑夜看见我而泪水涟涟？晨曦拥抱我便喜悦无限？

这可是真的？可是真的？你的爱穿越千年、跋涉万里把我来寻觅？

当你最终与我相遇，你地久天长的渴望是否找到完满的归宿？在我温柔的言语、双眼和双唇里，在我飘扬的头发里。

那么，我小小的额头上真的写着"无限"的神秘？

亲爱的，告诉我，这一切是否都是真的。

32

Tell me if this be all true, my lover, tell me if this be true.

When these eyes flash their lightning the dark clouds in your breast make stormy answer.

Is it true that my lips are sweet like the opening bud of the first conscious love?

Do the memories of vanished months of May linger in my limbs?

Does the earth, like a harp, shiver into songs with the touch of my feet?

Is it then true that the dewdrops fall from the eyes of night when I am seen, and the morning light is glad when it wraps my body round?

Is it true, is it true, that your love travelled alone through ages and worlds in search of me?

That when you found me at last, your age-long desire

found utter peace in my gentle speech and my eyes and lips and flowing hair?

Is it then true that the mystery of the Infinite is written on this little forehead of mine?

Tell me, my lover, if all this be true.

33

我爱你，心上人。请把我的爱原谅。

我像一只鸟迷失了方向，落入了情网。

当我的心摇荡，它滑落了面纱，一丝不挂。用怜悯遮住它吧，心上人，请把我的爱原谅。

如果你不能爱我，心上人，请把我的痛苦原谅。

不要远远地侧目，把我打量。

我将向隅而坐，黯然神伤。

我将双手掩面，羞愧难当。

转过你的面庞，心上人，请把我的痛苦原谅。

如果你爱我，心上人，请把我的欢乐原谅。

当我的心在幸福的洪流中随波逐浪，别让我危险的放纵贻笑大方。

当我坐在宝座上，以爱的专制对你颐指气使；当我像女神一样，赐你宠爱之时，请容忍我的趾高气扬，心上人，请把我的欢乐原谅。

33

I love you, beloved. Forgive me my love.

Like a bird losing its way I am caught.

When my heart was shaken it lost its veil and was naked.
Cover it with pity, beloved, and forgive me my love.

If you cannot love me, beloved, forgive me my pain.

Do not look askance at me from afar.

I will steal back to my corner and sit in the dark.

With both hands I will cover my naked shame.

Turn your face from me, beloved, and forgive me my
pain.

If you love me, beloved, forgive me my joy.

When my heart is borne away by the flood of happiness,
do not smile at my perilous abandonment.

When I sit on my throne and rule you with my tyranny of

love, when like a goddess I grant you my favour, bear with my pride, beloved, and forgive me my joy.

34

亲爱的，不要不辞而别。

我守候了一夜，如今已是睡意蒙眬。

唯恐你在我熟睡时一去无踪。

亲爱的，不要不辞而别。

我惊起伸出双手把你触碰，我喃喃自语："难道这是个梦？"

但愿我能用我的心缠住你的双足，紧紧抱在我的怀中！

亲爱的，不要不辞而别。

34

Do not go, my love, without asking my leave.

I have watched all night, and now my eyes are heavy with sleep.

I fear lest I lose you when I am sleeping.

Do not go, my love, without asking my leave.

I start up and stretch my hands to touch you. I ask myself, "Is it a dream?"

Could I but entangle your feet with my heart and hold them fast to my breast!

Do not go, my love, without asking my leave.

35

唯恐你我相识太匆匆，你便把我戏弄。
你用闪烁的笑声，掩盖你的泪光晶莹。
我懂，你的心计我懂，
你从不说出你的心声。

唯恐我不能捧你于掌中，你便千方百计地隐匿芳踪。
唯恐我把你和众人混淆不清，你便在一旁玉立亭亭。
我懂，你的心计我懂，
你从不敞开你的花径。

你的要求与众不同，因此你便缄默无声。
你用漫不经心的神情，回避了我的馈赠。
我懂，你的心计我懂，
你从不接受心之所钟。

35

Lest I should know you too easily, you play with me.

You blind me with flashes of laughter to hide your tears.

I know, I know your art,

You never say the word you would.

Lest I should not prize you, you elude me in a thousand ways.

Lest I should confuse you with the crowd, you stand aside.

I know, I know your art,

You never walk the path you would.

Your claim is more than that of others, that is why you are silent.

With playful carelessness you avoid my gifts.

I know, I know your art,

You never will take what you would.

36

他细语轻声："亲爱的，抬起你的眼睛。"

我厉声斥责他说："走开！"而他无动于衷。

他站在我的面前，握住我的双手。我说："放开我！"而他就是不走。

他把脸凑到我的耳边。我瞪了他一眼，说道："好不要脸！"而他就是不动弹。

他的双唇触碰我的脸。我浑身发抖，说道："你好大胆！"而他就是不怕羞。

他把一朵花戴在我的发间。我说："这有什么用！"而他站着一动不动。

他走了，取下了我颈上的花环。我泪流满面，问我的心："为何他一去不复返？"

36

He whispered, "My love, raise your eyes."

I sharply chid him, and said "Go!"; but he did not stir.

He stood before me and held both my hands. I said, "Leave me!"; but he did not go.

He brought his face near my ear. I glanced at him and said, "What a shame!"; but he did not move.

His lips touched my cheek. I trembled and said, "You dare too much"; but he had no shame.

He put a flower in my hair. I said, "It is useless!"; but he stood unmoved.

He took the garland from my neck and went away. I weep and ask my heart, "Why does he not come back?"

37

佳人，可否把你用鲜花编织的花环戴在我的颈上？

可是你要知道，我编织的那个花环，是为众人奉献——他们偶然闯入我的眼帘，或者住在尚未开发的家园，或者活在诗人的字里行间。

乞求心的交换，为时已晚。

我的生命曾经像花蕾一样，所有的芬芳都在花蕊里储藏。

而今已经消散在四面八方。

有谁懂得那种魔法，把它重新收集和封藏？

我的心，不为一人所有，愿为众人奉献。

37

Would you put your wreath of fresh flowers on my neck, fair one?

But you must know that the one wreath that I had woven is for the many, for those who are seen in glimpses, or dwell in lands unexplored, or live in poets' songs.

It is too late to ask my heart in return for yours.

There was a time when my life was like a bud, all its perfume was stored in its core.

Now it is squandered far and wide.

Who knows the enchantment that can gather and shut it up again?

My heart is not mine to give to one only, it is given to the many.

38

亲爱的，从前你的诗人在心里写下伟大的诗篇。

唉，我不小心，它碰到你叮当的脚镯而遭遇灾难。

它裂成诗歌的碎片，零乱地散落在你的脚边。

我所有关于往昔征战的篇章，在嘲笑的波浪中摇荡，最终浸没于泪行。

亲爱的，你必须对我的这一损失赔偿。

如果我不能在死后千古流芳，那就在生前给我以不朽的希望。

而我不会怪你，也不会因此而悲伤。

38

My love, once upon a time your poet launched a great epic in his mind.

Alas, I was not careful, and it struck your ringing anklets and came to grief.

It broke up into scraps of songs and lay scattered at your feet.

All my cargo of the stories of old wars was tossed by the laughing waves and soaked in tears and sank.

You must make this loss good to me, my love.

If my claims to immortal fame after death are shattered, make me immortal while I live.

And I will not mourn for my loss nor blame you.

39

整个早晨我想要编一个花环，可是花儿纷纷滑落。

你坐在那里，用眼角窥探着我。

问问这暗中策划恶作剧的双眼，究竟是谁的错。

我想放声歌唱，然而徒劳无功。

隐隐的笑容，在你的唇上颤动；仿佛在追问着我失败的隐情。

且让你微笑的双唇发誓：我的歌如何归于寂静无声，仿佛一只沉醉在荷花里的蜜蜂。

天色渐晚，花儿合起花瓣。

请允许我坐在你的身边，允许我的双唇做那些在沉默无声、星光朦胧中能做的事情。

39

I try to weave a wreath all the morning, but the flowers slip and they drop out.

You sit there watching me in secret through the corner of your prying eyes.

Ask those eyes, darkly planning mischief, whose fault it was.

I try to sing a song, but in vain.

A hidden smile trembles on your lips; ask of it the reason of my failure.

Let your smiling lips say on oath how my voice lost itself in silence like a drunken bee in the lotus.

It is evening, and the time for the flowers to close their petals.

Give me leave to sit by your side, and bid my lips to do

the work that can be done in silence and in the dim light of stars.

40

当我来向你告别的时候，一丝怀疑的微笑在你眼中闪过。

你认为我很快就会回来，因为我这样做的次数太多。

实话实说，我心里也有同样的疑惑。

因为春天去而复返，满月别过又圆，繁花羞红枝头，年复一年；我的告别可能只为了再回到你的身边。

且让这幻想片刻停留，不要粗暴地把它匆匆赶走。

当我说要永远离开你的时候，就当作真话来接受，让泪眼朦胧来暂时加深你黑色的眼影。

当我再回来的时候，任凭你的嬉笑嘲弄。

40

An unbelieving smile flits on your eyes when I come to you to take my leave.

I have done it so often that you think I will soon return.

To tell you the truth I have the same doubt in my mind.

For the spring days come again time after time; the full moon takes leave and comes on another visit, the flowers come again and blush upon their branches year after year, and it is likely that I take my leave only to come to you again.

But keep the illusion awhile; do not send it away with ungentle haste.

When I say I leave you for all time, accept it as true, and let a mist of tears for one moment deepen the dark rim of your eyes.

Then smile as archly as you like when I come again.

41

我想对你说，不得不说的最深情的许诺；而我却不敢说，因为怕你嘲笑我。

这便是我为何自嘲，在玩笑中把心里的秘密打破。

我对我的痛苦轻描淡写，因为怕你这样做。

我想对你说，不得不说的最真实的许诺；而我却不敢说，因为怕你不相信我。

这便是为何我言不由衷，真话假说。

我对我的痛苦哭笑不得，因为怕你这样做。

我想用最珍贵的词语把你言说；而我却不敢说，因为怕你不用相应的词语回应我。

这便是为何我对你恶语相加，并夸耀自己的冷漠。

我伤你的心，因为怕你永远不知道痛苦是什么。

我想静静地坐在你的身畔；而我却不敢，怕我的心会跳到我的唇边。

这便是为何我轻松地东拉西扯，把我的心藏在言语的后面。

我粗鲁地对待我的痛苦，因为怕你这样做。

我想离开你的身边；而我却不敢，怕我的懦弱被你发现。

这便是为何我昂首挺胸漫不经心地走到你的面前。

你的目光频频如电，使我的痛苦永远新鲜。

41

I long to speak the deepest words I have to say to you; but I dare not, for fear you should laugh.

That is why I laugh at myself and shatter my secret in jest.

I make light of my pain, afraid you should do so.

I long to tell you the truest words I have to say to you; but I dare not, being afraid that you would not believe them.

That is why I disguise them in untruth, saying the contrary of what I mean.

I make my pain appear absurd, afraid that you should do so.

I long to use the most precious words I have for you; but I dare not, fearing I should not be paid with like value.

That is why I give you hard names and boast of my callous strength.

I hurt you, for fear you should never know any pain.

I long to sit silent by you; but I dare not lest my heart come out at my lips.

That is why I prattle and chatter lightly and hide my heart behind words.

I rudely handle my pain, for fear you should do so.

I long to go away from your side; but I dare not, for fear my cowardice should become known to you.

That is why I hold my head high and carelessly come into your presence.

Constant thrusts from your eyes keep my pain fresh for ever.

42

疯了呵，喝得烂醉如泥；

如果你踢开大门，当众作傻装痴；

如果你在一夜之间囊空如洗，对于节俭谨慎嗤之以鼻；

如果你走稀奇古怪的路，玩着毫无用处的东西；

莫名其妙，毫无道理；

如果你在风暴来临前扬帆，却把船舵折为两半，

那么我会跟随你，朋友，烂醉如泥，一蹶不起。

我和稳重聪明的邻居朝夕相处消磨时间；

苦学令我渐生华发，细察令我目视昏花。

多年以来我已积攒了不少断简残编：

把这些东西撕碎吧，然后在上面起舞，丢到风中飘散。

因为我知道，智慧的登峰造极就是烂醉如泥，一蹶
不起。

且让一切扭曲的顾虑消亡，让我无望地迷失方向。

且让一阵旋风袭来，把我从锚上卷走。

世上满是大人物和劳工，能干且聪明。

有些人从容在前，有些人甘居人后。

且让他们幸福而成功，而我傻乎乎地徒劳无功。

因为我知道，所有工作的结局都是烂醉如泥，一蹶不起。

我发誓在此刻向体面的上等人放弃一切要求。

我放弃博学多才的自豪和明辨是非的骄傲。

我要打碎记忆的容器，抛洒最后的泪滴。

我要在浆果红酒的泡沫里沐浴，让欢笑熠熠生辉。

我暂且把文质彬彬的标签撕得粉碎。

我发誓将一文不值，烂醉如泥，一蹶不起。

O mad, superbly drunk;

If you kick open your doors and play the fool in public;

If you empty your bag in a night, and snap your fingers at prudence;

If you walk in curious paths and play with useless things;

Reck not rhyme or reason;

If unfurling your sails before the storm you snap the rudder in two,

Then I will follow you, comrade, and be drunken and go to the dogs.

I have wasted my days and nights in the company of steady wise neighbours.

Much knowing has turned my hair grey, and much watching has made my sight dim.

For years I have gathered and heaped up scraps and

fragments of things:

Crush them and dance upon them, and scatter them all to the winds.

For I know 'tis the height of wisdom to be drunken and go to the dogs.

Let all crooked scruples vanish, let me hopelessly lose my way.

Let a gust of wild giddiness come and sweep me away from my anchors.

The world is peopled with worthies, and workers, useful and clever.

There are men who are easily first, and men who come decently after.

Let them be happy and prosper, and let me be foolishly futile.

For I know 'tis the end of all works to be drunken and go to the dogs.

I swear to surrender this moment all claims to the ranks of the decent.

I let go my pride of learning and judgment of right and of wrong.

I'll shatter memory's vessel, scattering the last drop of tears.

With the foam of the berry-red wine I will bathe and brighten my laughter.

The badge of the civil and staid I'll tear into shreds for the nonce.

I'll take the holy vow to be worthless, to be drunken and go to the dogs.

43

不，朋友，不管你怎么说，我决不做个苦行僧。

如果她不和我一起立誓发声，我决不做个苦行僧。

这是我的决定，如果我找不到荫蔽之所并结伴苦行，我决不做个苦行僧。

不，朋友，如果林荫中没有欢笑的回声，如果风中没有飘扬的橘黄色的披风，如果柔声细语没有让森林愈发寂静，我决不离开我的家庭，决不退隐在这孤寂的林中。

我决不做个苦行僧。

43

No, my friends, I shall never be an ascetic, whatever you may say.

I shall never be an ascetic if she does not take the vow with me.

It is my firm resolve that if I cannot find a shady shelter and a companion for my penance, I shall never turn ascetic.

No, my friends, I shall never leave my hearth and home, and retire into the forest solitude, if rings no merry laughter in its echoing shade and if the end of no saffron mantle flutters in the wind; if its silence is not deepened by soft whispers.

I shall never be an ascetic.

44

长老，饶恕这一对罪人吧。今天的春风狂野地奔腾，卷走了尘土和枯叶，你的教训也随之消失无踪。

长老，不要说人生虚空。

因为我们一度与死亡签署停战协定，我俩仅在这几个芬芳的时辰里获得了永生。

哪怕国王的军队前来向我们猛烈地进攻，我们也要悲哀地摇头，说："兄弟们，你们扰乱了我们的安宁。如果你们一定要玩这吵闹的游戏，请去别处把你们的武器摆弄。因为我们在这稍纵即逝的瞬间里获得了永生。"

如果友善的人们前来把我们围拢，我们也要谦逊地向他们鞠躬，说："意外的荣幸陷我们于窘境。在我们居住的无垠天空，没有多余的地方。因为春天里繁花怒放，蜜蜂忙碌的翅膀彼此冲撞。只容我俩永生的地方，是我们无比狭窄的小小的天堂。"

44

Reverend sir, forgive this pair of sinners. Spring winds to-day are blowing in wild eddies, driving dust and dead leaves away, and with them your lessons are all lost.

Do not say, father, that life is a vanity.

For we have made truce with death for once, and only for a few fragrant hours we two have been made immortal.

Even if the king's army came and fiercely fell upon us we should sadly shake our heads and say, Brothers, you are disturbing us. If you must have this noisy game, go and clatter your arms elsewhere. Since only for a few fleeting moments we have been made immortal.

If friendly people came and flocked around us, we should humbly bow to them and say, This extravagant good fortune is an embarrassment to us. Room is scarce in the infinite sky where we dwell. For in the springtime flowers come in crowds, and the busy wings of bees jostle each other. Our little heaven, where dwell only we two immortals, is too absurdly narrow.

45

祝福要离开的宾朋一路顺风，了无遗踪。

带着笑容，把轻松、单纯和亲近的都抱在怀中。

今天的节日属于幻影，它们不知道何始何终。

且让你的笑声只是毫无意义的欢畅，正如涟漪上闪耀的波光。

且让你的生命在时光的边缘上轻舞飞扬，宛如叶尖上的露珠一样。

且在你竖琴的弦上，弹奏出转瞬而逝的断续的乐章。

45

To the guests that must go bid God's speed and brush away all traces of their steps.

Take to your bosom with a smile what is easy and simple and near.

To-day is the festival of phantoms that know not when they die.

Let your laughter be but a meaningless mirth like twinkles of light on the ripples.

Let your life lightly dance on the edges of Time like dew on the tip of a leaf.

Strike in chords from your harp fitful momentary rhythms.

46

你离开我扬长而去。

我想我应该为你哀伤，用金色的诗行把你孤寂的形象刻在我心上。

唉，倒霉的我，短暂的时光。

韶华年复一年地蹉跎；春日不堪消磨；柔弱的花朵莫名地凋落，而智者告诫我说，生命不过是荷叶上的一颗露珠。

我是否应该忽视这一切，目送她转身离开我？

那样既粗鲁又愚蠢，因为时光短暂哦。

那么，来吧，我的雨声淅沥的夜晚；微笑吧，我的金色的秋天；来吧，无忧无虑的四月天，把你的爱广为流传。

来吧，还有你，你也来吧！

亲爱的，你们知道我们都很平凡。为带走她的心的人而心碎，是明智之举吗？因为时光短暂呵。

坐在角落里冥思，用诗写下你是我的全部，这样很甜蜜。

拥抱自己的忧伤，决不受人安慰，这样充满英雄气。

而一张新鲜的脸庞，在我门外偷窥，抬眼与我凝眸相对。

我只好拭去眼泪，改弦更张。

因为这短暂的时光。

46

You left me and went on your way.

I thought I should mourn for you and set your solitary image in my heart wrought in a golden song.

But ah, my evil fortune, time is short.

Youth wanes year after year; the spring days are fugitive; the frail flowers die for nothing, and the wise man warns me that life is but a dewdrop on the lotus leaf.

Should I neglect all this to gaze after one who has turned her back on me?

That would be rude and foolish, for time is short.

Then, come, my rainy nights with pattering feet; smile, my golden autumn; come, careless April, scattering your kisses abroad.

You come, and you, and you also!

My loves, you know we are mortals. Is it wise to break one's heart for the one who takes her heart away? For time is short.

It is sweet to sit in a corner to muse and write in rhymes that you are all my world.

It is heroic to hug one's sorrow and determine not to be consoled.

But a fresh face peeps across my door and raises its eyes to my eyes.

I cannot but wipe away my tears and change the tune of my song.

For time is short.

47

如果你要这样，我便停止歌唱。

如果我的凝视使你的心荡漾，我便把目光移出你的脸庞。

如果我的突然出现使你惊慌，我便另辟蹊径，离开你的身旁。

如果我的出现令编织花环的你心烦意乱，我便避开你孤寂的花园。

如果我的小舟使得水花飞溅，我便不会泛舟于你的岸边。

47

If you would have it so, I will end my singing.

If it sets your heart aflutter, I will take away my eyes from your face.

If it suddenly startles you in your walk, I will step aside and take another path.

If it confuses you in your flower-weaving, I will shun your lonely garden.

If it makes the water wanton and wild, I will not row my boat by your bank.

48

亲爱的，松开你柔情蜜意的网！这亲吻的酒已令我过量。

浓香的雾塞满了我的心房。

敞开门吧，为晨曦腾出地方。

我在你身上迷失了方向，在你层层包裹的爱抚中徜徉。

收了你的魔法吧，把我释放，还我阳刚，把我获得自由的心为你奉上。

48

Free me from the bonds of your sweetness, my love! No more of this wine of kisses.

This mist of heavy incense stifles my heart.

Open the doors, make room for the morning light.

I am lost in you, wrapped in the folds of your caresses.

Free me from your spells, and give me back the manhood to offer you my freed heart.

49

我握住她的手，把她紧抱在怀中。

我想怀抱着她的美貌花容，亲吻着她嫣然的笑容，沉醉于她顾盼生辉的眼睛。

呵，可是，美在哪里？谁能把蔚蓝剥离出碧空？

我想要抓住美的身影；而它把我捉弄，只留下躯体在我的手中。

只有灵魂可以触碰的花朵，躯体怎能触碰？

49

I hold her hands and press her to my breast.

I try to fill my arms with her loveliness, to plunder her sweet smile with kisses, to drink her dark glances with my eyes.

Ah, but, where is it? Who can strain the blue from the sky?

I try to grasp the beauty; it eludes me, leaving only the body in my hands.

Baffled and weary I come back.

How can the body touch the flower which only the spirit may touch?

50

亲爱的，与你相会令我朝思暮想——它仿佛是吞噬一切的死亡。

它让我一无所有，仿佛风暴席卷八荒；它让我辗转反侧，醒来一枕黄粱。

在这毁灭里，在这精神的袒露无遗里，让我们在美之中合二为一。

唉，我虚妄的欲望！我的神，除了在你那里，哪儿有合二为一的希望？

50

Love, my heart longs day and night for the meeting with you—for the meeting that is like all-devouring death.

Sweep me away like a storm; take everything I have; break open my sleep and plunder my dreams. Rob me of my world.

In that devastation, in the utter nakedness of spirit, let us become one in beauty.

Alas for my vain desire! Where is this hope for union except in thee, my God?

51

当曲终人散，夜色阑珊，且让我们各踏归程，忘却今宵的梦。

我欲揽谁入怀中？总是好梦难成。

此情殷勤却成空，惆怅填膺。

51

Then finish the last song and let us leave.

Forget this night when the night is no more.

Whom do I try to clasp in my arms? Dreams can never be made captive.

My eager hands press emptiness to my heart and it bruises my breast.

52

为什么灯灭了?

我用披风遮住灯挡住风,结果灯灭了。

为什么花谢了?

我用热烈的爱把花压在心中,结果花谢了。

为什么溪水干了?

我在溪上筑坝拦水私用,结果溪水干了。

为什么琴弦断了?

我试图强弹一个音符而它力不能胜,结果琴弦断了。

52

Why did the lamp go out?

I shaded it with my cloak to save it from the wind, that is why the lamp went out.

Why did the flower fade?

I pressed it to my heart with anxious love, that is why the flower faded.

Why did the stream dry up?

I put a dam across it to have it for my use, that is why the stream dried up.

Why did the harp-string break?

I tried to force a note that was beyond its power, that is why the harp-string is broken.

53

为何你令我自惭形秽，只因那一瞥？

我并非一个乞者。

我只不过站在你的院边篱外，逗留了一时半刻。

为何你令我自惭形秽，只因那一瞥？

我没有从你的园中采一朵花、摘一颗果。

我谦卑地躲在路边的树荫下——每个陌生旅人的驻足
之所。

我一朵玫瑰也没有采撷。

唉，我走累了，而骤雨又落。

风在呼啸，竹林摇曳。

云层仿佛溃散而逃，横空而过。

我走累了。

我不知道你如何看我，也不知道你在门口等谁呢。

闪电令你目不暇接。

我怎么知道你看得见站在黑暗中的我？

我不知道你如何看我。

白昼终结，骤雨初歇。

我把树荫留在花园深处，那片草地我曾经坐过。

天色已晚；关上门吧；我去意已决。

白昼终结了。

53

Why do you put me to shame with a look?

I have not come as a beggar.

Only for a passing hour I stood at the end of your courtyard outside the garden hedge.

Why do you put me to shame with a look?

Not a rose did I gather from your garden, not a fruit did I pluck.

I humbly took my shelter under the wayside shade where every strange traveller may stand.

Not a rose did I pluck.

Yes, my feet were tired, and the shower of rain came down.

The winds cried out among the swaying bamboo branches.

The clouds ran across the sky as though in the flight from

defeat.

My feet were tired.

I know not what you thought of me or for whom you were waiting at your door.

Flashes of lightning dazzled your watching eyes.

How could I know that you could see me where I stood in the dark?

I know not what you thought of me.

The day is ended, and the rain has ceased for a moment.

I leave the shadow of the tree at the end of your garden and this seat on the grass.

It has darkened; shut your door;   I go my way.

The day is ended.

54

当集市关门、夜色深沉，你提着篮子匆匆地要去哪里？

他们都背着东西回家去了；月亮从树梢上面窥视着村子。

呼唤摆渡的回音，越过幽暗的水面，飘向远处野鸭沉睡的沼泽地。

当集市关门，你提着篮子匆匆地要去哪里？

大地睡眼迷离。

鸦巢已归于沉寂，萧萧竹叶也已无语。

从田里归来的劳动的人们，在院子里摊开了蒲席。

当集市关门，你提着篮子匆匆地要去哪里？

54

Where do you hurry with your basket this late evening when the marketing is over?

They all have come home with their burdens; the moon peeps from above the village trees.

The echoes of the voices calling for the ferry run across the dark water to the distant swamp where wild ducks sleep.

Where do you hurry with your basket when the marketing is over?

Sleep has laid her fingers upon the eyes of the earth.

The nests of the crows have become silent, and the murmurs of the bamboo leaves are silent.

The labourers home from their fields spread their mats in the courtyards.

Where do you hurry with your basket when the marketing is over?

正午时分，你悄然离去。

火伞高张。

当你离去的时候，我已忙完了活计，独坐在阳台上。

阵阵疾风撷来远方田野的芬芳。

鸽子在树荫里不倦地柔声细语；蜜蜂误入我的房里，哼唱着远方田野的消息。

村庄在正午的炎热里睡去。路上空空荡荡。

树叶的萧萧声此消彼长。

当村庄在正午的炎热里睡去，我凝望着天空，在那片蔚蓝里编织着我熟悉的那个人的名字。

我忘记了把头发编起。慵懒的风儿在我的脸颊上与它嬉戏。

绿树成荫的河岸下，河水静静地流淌。

懒洋洋的白云挂在天上。

我忘记了把头发编起。

正午时分，你悄然离去。

路上尘土炽热，田野气喘吁吁。

鸽子在密叶间柔声细语。

当你离去的时候，我独坐在阳台上。

55

It was mid-day when you went away.

The sun was strong in the sky.

I had done my work and sat alone on my balcony when you went away.

Fitful gusts came winnowing through the smells of many distant fields.

The doves cooed tireless in the shade, and a bee strayed in my room humming the news of many distant fields.

The village slept in the noonday heat. The road lay deserted.

In sudden fits the rustling of the leaves rose and died.

I gazed at the sky and wove in the blue the letters of a name I had known, while the village slept in the noonday heat.

I had forgotten to braid my hair. The languid breeze played with it upon my cheek.

The river ran unruffled under the shady bank.

The lazy white clouds did not move.

I had forgotten to braid my hair.

It was mid-day when you went away.

The dust of the road was hot and the fields panting.

The doves cooed among the dense leaves.

I was alone in my balcony when you went away.

56

众多女人忙于平淡无奇的日常家务活，我不过是其中一个。

为何你单把我挑出来，带我离开平凡生活凉爽的荫蔽之所？

圣洁的爱不善表达。它在隐藏的心底幽暗里，如宝石般闪耀着光华。在奇异的日光下，它却暗淡得可怜巴巴。

呵，你闯入我的心扉，把我颤抖的爱拖到光天化日之下，永远摧毁了它藏身的隐蔽的家。

其他的女人一如往昔。

没有人窥探她们的心底，她们也不了解自己的秘密。

她们淡淡地微笑，轻轻地哭泣；扯着闲篇，忙着活计。她们拜佛，点灯，汲水，日复一日。

我希望我的爱能从无处藏身的颤抖的羞耻中救赎，而你却转身而去。

　　唉，你的面前是阳关大路，而你却断了我的归途，让我在这个世界面前被日夜凝视，一览无余。

56

I was one among many women busy with the obscure daily tasks of the household.

Why did you single me out and bring me away from the cool shelter of our common life?

Love unexpressed is sacred. It shines like gems in the gloom of the hidden heart. In the light of the curious day it looks pitifully dark.

Ah, you broke through the cover of my heart and dragged my trembling love into the open place, destroying for ever the shady corner where it hid its nest.

The other women are the same as ever.

No one has peeped into their inmost being, and they themselves know not their own secret.

Lightly they smile, and weep, chatter, and work. Daily

they go to the temple, light their lamps, and fetch water from the river.

I hoped my love would be saved from the shivering shame of the shelterless, but you turn your face away.

Yes, your path lies open before you, but you have cut off my return, and left me stripped naked before the world with its lidless eyes staring night and day.

57

世界呵，我采了你的花朵。

我把它埋在心里，而它却刺痛了我。

当天色渐暗，我发现花已凋谢，而痛苦依然。

世界呵，更多的芬芳绽放的花朵将来到你身边。

而我的采花时代结束了，长夜漫漫，我没有玫瑰相伴，而痛苦依然。

57

I plucked your flower, O world!

I pressed it to my heart and the thorn pricked.

When the day waned and it darkened, I found that the flower had faded, but the pain remained.

More flowers will come to you with perfume and pride, O world!

But my time for flower-gathering is over, and through the dark night I have not my rose, only the pain remains.

58

一天早晨，在花园里，一个盲女孩献给我一串用荷叶覆盖的花环。

我把花环套在颈上，不禁泪水涟涟。

我吻了她，说："你和花一样，美丽却视而不见。"

58

One morning in the flower garden a blind girl came to offer me a flower chain in the cover of a lotus leaf.

I put it round my neck, and tears came to my eyes.

I kissed her and said, "You are blind even as the flowers are.

"You yourself know not how beautiful is your gift."

59

女人呵，你不仅是上帝的杰作，也是男人的杰作；你永远美丽，在他们的心上。

诗人用梦幻般的金线为你编织诗行；画家为你描绘永远新鲜永恒的形象。

大海把珍珠献上，矿山把黄金献上，夏日的花园用繁花为你梳妆，为你披上霓裳，让你珍贵异常。

男人心中的欲望，曾在你的青春里洒下光芒。

你一半是女人，一半是梦想。

59

O woman, you are not merely the handiwork of God, but also of men; these are ever endowing you with beauty from their hearts.

Poets are weaving for you a web with threads of golden imagery; painters are giving your form ever new immortality.

The sea gives its pearls, the mines their gold, the summer gardens their flowers to deck you, to cover you, to make you more precious.

The desire of men's hearts has shed its glory over your youth.

You are one half woman and one half dream.

60

在人生的匆忙与喧哗之间，一成不变的美呵，静静地站立，孤独而超然。

美好的时光沉醉在你的脚边，低语喃喃：

"亲爱的，说吧，对我说吧；我的新娘，说吧。"

永恒的美呵，你却闭口无言。

60

Amidst the rush and roar of life, O Beauty, carved in stone, you stand mute and still, alone and aloof.

Great Time sits enamoured at your feet and murmurs:

"Speak, speak to me, my love; speak, my bride!"

But your speech is shut up in stone, O Immovable Beauty!

61

我的心，安静吧，且让这离别的时刻变得甜蜜。

且让这离别不是结束，而是圆满。

且让爱恋化作回忆，痛苦化作诗篇。

且让穿越天空的飞翔敛翅，回归家园。

且让你双手的最后一抹温柔，如夜花一样娇软。

哦，美丽的结局，请静立在这瞬间，默默地把别语倾诉。

我向你鞠躬，举起灯，为你照亮前路。

61

Peace, my heart, let the time for the parting be sweet.

Let it not be a death but completeness.

Let love melt into memory and pain into songs.

Let the flight through the sky end in the folding of the wings over the nest.

Let the last touch of your hands be gentle like the flower of the night.

Stand still, O Beautiful End, for a moment, and say your last words in silence.

I bow you and hold up my lamp to light you on your way.

62

在梦中的朦胧小径，我去找寻前生的爱情。

她的家坐落在一条荒凉街道的尽头。

晚风中，她宠爱的孔雀在栖枝上睡意蒙眬，而鸽子在自己的角落里沉默无声。

她在大门口放下灯，在我面前玉立亭亭。

她抬起大眼睛，看着我的脸，却沉默无声："你好吗，我的朋友？"

我想要开口，我们却相顾忘言。

我左思右想，却记不起我们的姓名。

她的眼中泪光闪烁晶莹。她向我伸出右手。我握住她的手，伫立无声。

我们的灯摇曳着，熄灭在晚风中。

62

In the dusky path of a dream I went to seek the love who was mine in a former life.

Her house stood at the end of a desolate street.

In the evening breeze her pet peacock sat drowsing on its perch, and the pigeons were silent in their corner.

She set her lamp down by the portal and stood before me.

She raised her large eyes to my face and mutely asked, "Are you well, my friend?"

I tried to answer, but our language had been lost and forgotten.

I thought and thought; our names would not come to my mind.

Tears shone in her eyes. She held up her right hand to me.

I took it and stood silent.

Our lamp had flickered in the evening breeze and died.

63

你一定要走吗，旅人？

夜深人静，黑暗笼罩着森林。

露台上灯火通明，繁花似锦，年轻的眼睛依然清醒。

是不是到了离别时分？

你一定要走吗，旅人？

我们不曾以恳求的手臂来束缚你的脚步前行。

大门敞开。你的马已备好鞍，立在门外。

如果我们曾设法拦住你的去路，也不过是用我们的歌声。

如果我们曾设法把你挽留，也不过是用我们凝视的眼睛。

旅人，我们没有办法把你留住。我们只有泪水纵横。

是什么不熄之火闪烁在你的眼中？

是什么不安的狂热在你的血液里奔腾？

是什么召唤在黑暗中把你驱动？

在满天的繁星中，你看出了什么可怕的咒语，黑夜带着密封的消息，进入了你沉默而陌生的心灵？

疲惫的心呵，如果你不爱欢乐的聚会，如果你需要安静，我们便熄灭灯火，停下琴声。

我们便静坐在风叶萧萧的黑暗中，看那疲倦的月儿把苍白的清辉洒在你的窗棂。

旅人呵，是什么不眠的精灵从午夜的心中把你触碰？

63

Traveller, must you go?

The night is still and the darkness swoons upon the forest.

The lamps are bright in our balcony, the flowers all fresh, and the youthful eyes still awake.

Is the time for your parting come?

Traveller, must you go?

We have not bound your feet with our entreating arms.

Your doors are open. Your horse stands saddled at the gate.

If we have tried to bar your passage it was but with our songs.

Did we ever try to hold you back it was but with our eyes.

Traveller, we are helpless to keep you. We have only our tears.

What quenchless fire glows in your eyes?

What restless fever runs in your blood?

What call from the dark urges you?

What awful incantation have you read among the stars in the sky, that with a sealed secret message the night entered your heart, silent and strange?

If you do not care for merry meetings, if you must have peace, weary heart, we shall put our lamps out and silence our harps.

We shall sit still in the dark in the rustle of leaves, and the tired moon will shed pale rays on your window.

O traveller, what sleepless spirit has touched you from the heart of the midnight?

白天我跋涉在路上，满身灼热的灰尘。

而今，在黄昏的凉意里，我敲着颓败荒凉客栈的门。

一棵阴森的菩提树饥饿的树根，在颓垣的裂缝里紧紧
延伸。

曾有这样的日子——徒步的旅人来到这里洗去征尘。

他们沐浴着初升的朦胧月光，在院里铺开席子，坐下
来谈论着异乡。

清晨，他们醒来时神清气爽，鸟儿欢唱，友善的花儿
恭候在路旁。

而我到来的时候，却没有守候的灯火点亮。

只有遗弃的残灯，在墙上留下熏黑的污痕，仿佛盲人
凝视的眼睛。

干涸池边丛中的流萤浮光掠影，竹影横斜在碧草如茵
的小径。

白昼已尽，我是孤独的旅人。

面前长夜漫漫，而我已疲惫不堪。

I spent my day on the scorching hot dust of the road.

Now, in the cool of the evening, I knock at the door of the inn. It is deserted and in ruins.

A grim *ashath* tree spreads its hungry clutching roots through the gaping fissures of the walls.

Days have been when wayfarers came here to wash their weary feet.

They spread their mats in the courtyard in the dim light of the early moon, and sat and talked of strange lands.

They woke refreshed in the morning when birds made them glad, and friendly flowers nodded their heads at them from the wayside.

But no lighted lamp awaited me when I came here.

The black smudges of smoke left by many a forgotten evening lamp stare, like blind eyes, from the wall.

Fireflies flit in the bush near the dried-up pond, and bamboo branches fling their shadows on the grass-grown path.

I am the guest of no one at the end of my day.

The long night is before me, and I am tired.

65

那是你的再一次呼唤？

夜幕降临。疲倦仿佛求爱的手臂把我纠缠。

是你在把我呼唤？

残忍的情人，我已把整个白天为你奉献，你一定还要
剥夺我的夜晚？

凡事总有个完，黑暗的孤寂属于自己独占。

你的声音一定要划破黑暗，使我深感不安？

难道夜晚没有留下催眠的音乐在你的大门？

难道从来没有攀登无情之塔上空的无声星辰？

难道你花园里的花朵永远不会零落成尘？

你这不安的人，你一定要把我呼唤？

那就让爱的泪眼，徒劳把秋水望穿。

且在孤寂的房中把灯点燃。

且把疲惫的劳工送上归船。

我把梦抛在身后，来奔赴你的召唤。

65

Is that your call again?

The evening has come. Weariness clings round me like the arms of entreating love.

Do you call me?

I had given all my day to you, cruel mistress, must you also rob me of my night?

Somewhere there is an end to everything, and the loneness of the dark is one's own.

Must your voice cut through it and smite me?

Has the evening no music of sleep at your gate?

Do the silent-winged stars never climb the sky above your pitiless tower?

Do the flowers never drop on the dust in soft death in your garden?

Must you call me, you unquiet one?

Then let the sad eyes of love vainly watch and weep.

Let the lamp burn in the lonely house.

Let the ferry-boat take the weary labourers to their home.

I leave behind my dreams and I hasten to your call.

66

　　一个流浪的疯子在把试金石寻找，他蜡黄的沾满灰尘的头发像堆乱草，骨瘦形销，形影相吊；他紧闭的双唇，仿佛他紧闭的心扉；他燃烧的眼睛，好像萤火虫寻觅伴侣的灯。

　　无垠的大海在他面前咆哮。

　　絮絮叨叨的海浪滔滔不绝地谈论着隐藏的珠宝，把莫名其妙的无知的人们嘲笑。

　　也许他现在希望渺茫，然而他却不肯罢休，因为这种寻找已经成为他的生命——

　　正如大海永远举起臂膀，伸向遥不可及的天空——

　　正如星辰周而复始的运行，却在追求永远不能达到的目标——

　　然而那头发脏乱的疯子依旧徘徊在孤寂的海滩上，把试金石寻找。

有一天，一个乡下男孩走过来问道："告诉我，你腰间的那条金链子是从哪里找到？"

疯子瞪大了眼睛——那条原本是铁的链子变成了真金；这不是梦境，然而他却不知道变化在何时发生。

他狂乱地捶着额头——哦，他在哪里不知不觉中获得了成功？

这已经变成了一种习惯——捡起石头，把链子触碰，然后又把石头扔掉，也不看是否有变化发生；疯子就这样，把试金石得而复失。

太阳西沉，晚霞如金。

疯子循着自己的脚印，像一棵被连根拔起的树，重新把失去的珠宝找寻，他驼背弯腰，精疲力竭，心也零落成尘。

66

A wandering madman was seeking the touchstone, with matted locks, tawny and dust-laden, and body worn to a shadow, his lips tight-pressed, like the shut-up doors of his heart, his burning eyes like the lamp of a glow-worm seeking its mate.

Before him the endless ocean roared.

The garrulous waves ceaselessly talked of hidden treasures, mocking the ignorance that knew not their meaning.

Maybe he now had no hope remaining, yet he would not rest, for the search had become his life,—

Just as the ocean for ever lifts its arms to the sky for the unattainable—

Just as the stars go in circles, yet seeking a goal that can never be reached—

Even so on the lonely shore the madman with dusty tawny

locks still roamed in search of the touchstone.

One day a village boy came up and asked, "Tell me, where did you come at this golden chain about your waist?"

The madman started—the chain that once was iron was verily gold; it was not a dream, but he did not know when it had changed.

He struck his forehead wildly—where, O where had he without knowing it achieved success?

It had grown into a habit, to pick up pebbles and touch the chain, and to throw them away without looking to see if a change had come; thus the madman found and lost the touchstone.

The sun was sinking low in the west, the sky was of gold.

The madman returned on his footsteps to seek anew the lost treasure, with his strength gone, his body bent, and his heart in the dust, like a tree uprooted.

67

虽然夜晚脚步蹒跚，已经示意所有歌声走向终点；

虽然你的同伴已回去休息，而你也已疲倦；

虽然恐惧在黑暗中弥漫，天空的脸也被遮掩；

可是，鸟儿呵，我的鸟儿呵，听我说，不要收起你的翅膀。

那不是林中树叶的幽暗，那是像黑蛇一样起伏的海洋。

那不是绽放的素馨花的舞姿，那是泡沫的闪光。

啊，何处是阳光明媚的绿色海岸，何处是你的家园？

鸟儿呵，我的鸟儿呵，听我说，不要收起你的翅膀。

孤寂的夜晚躺在你的小径上，黎明在幽暗的群山之后酣眠。

繁星屏息计算着时间，柔弱的月儿在深夜中游荡。

鸟儿呵，我的鸟儿呵，听我说，不要收起你的翅膀。

对于你，没有希望，没有恐惧。

没有言辞，没有低语，没有哭泣。

没有家，没有休息的床。

只有你自己的一双翅膀，以及无路的穹苍。

鸟儿呵，我的鸟儿呵，听我说，不要收起你的翅膀。

67

Though the evening comes with slow steps and has signalled for all songs to cease;

Though your companions have gone to their rest and you are tired;

Though fear broods in the dark and the face of the sky is veiled;

Yet, bird, O my bird, listen to me, do not close your wings.

That is not the gloom of the leaves of the forest, that is the sea swelling like a dark black snake.

That is not the dance of the flowering jasmine, that is flashing foam.

Ah, where is the sunny green shore, where is your nest?

Bird, O my bird, listen to me, do not close your wings.

The lone night lies along your path, the dawn sleeps

behind the shadowy hills.

The stars hold their breath counting the hours, the feeble moon swims the deep night.

Bird, O my bird, listen to me, do not close your wings.

There is no hope, no fear for you.

There is no word, no whisper, no cry.

There is no home, no bed of rest.

There is only your own pair of wings and the pathless sky.

Bird, O my bird, listen to me, do not close your wings.

68

兄弟，没有人可以永生，没有什么可以长存。且铭记在心，乐在其中。

我们的生活不是一种陈旧的负重，我们的道路不是一段漫长的旅程。

一个独特的诗人，不必为一首老歌吟唱。

花儿枯萎凋零；而戴花的人不必为它永远哀伤。

兄弟，且铭记在心，乐在其中。

必须有一个完整的暂停，才能将完美与音乐交融。

生命终将迟暮，沉浸于金色的阴影中。

必须让爱情不再游戏人生，且让它痛饮悲伤，携来泪的天堂。

兄弟，且铭记在心，乐在其中。

我们匆匆采集花朵，唯恐被路过的风掠夺。

抓住稍纵即逝的热吻，会使我们热血沸腾，目光炯炯。

热切的生命，强烈的渴望，时间在敲响离别的钟声。

兄弟，且铭记在心，乐在其中。

我们无暇把一件事物抓紧，揉碎，再弃于地上。

飞逝的时光，把梦想隐藏。

人生短促，只不过几天恋爱的韶光。

若只为工作与苦差，生命则将是无尽的漫长。

兄弟，且铭记在心，乐在其中。

美对我们来说是甜蜜的，因为她和我们的生活一起，随着转瞬即逝的旋律轻舞飞扬。

知识对我们来说是珍贵的，因为我们永远来不及使其臻于完满。

一切都完成于永恒的天堂。

而大地的幻象之花，因死亡而永葆新鲜。

兄弟，且铭记在心，乐在其中。

68

None lives for ever, brother, and nothing lasts for long. Keep that in mind and rejoice.

Our life is not the one old burden, our path is not the one long journey.

One sole poet has not to sing one aged song.

The flower fades and dies; but he who wears the flower has not to mourn for it for ever.

Brother, keep that in mind and rejoice.

There must come a full pause to weave perfection into music.

Life droops toward its sunset to be drowned in the golden shadows.

Love must be called from its play to drink sorrow and be borne to the heaven of tears.

Brother, keep that in mind and rejoice.

We hasten to gather our flowers lest they are plundered by the passing winds.

It quickens our blood and brightens our eyes to snatch kisses that would vanish if we delayed.

Our life is eager, our desires are keen, for time tolls the bell of parting.

Brother, keep that in mind and rejoice.

There is not time for us to clasp a thing and crush it and fling it away to the dust.

The hours trip rapidly away, hiding their dreams in their skirts.

Our life is short; it yields but a few days for love.

Were it for work and drudgery it would be endlessly long.

Brother, keep that in mind and rejoice.

Beauty is sweet to us, because she dances to the same fleeting tune with our lives.

Knowledge is precious to us, because we shall never have time to complete it.

All is done and finished in the eternal Heaven.

But earth's flowers of illusion are kept eternally fresh by death.

Brother, keep that in mind and rejoice.

69

我追寻金鹿。

朋友们，你们也许会笑，而我追求的愿景无法抵达。

我穿越山丘峡谷，浪迹无名的国土，因为我在追寻金鹿。

你来到集市上购物，满载归家；而无家可归的风，不知在何时何地使我中了魔法。

我心中了无牵挂；我把所有的一切都远远地抛下。

我穿越山丘峡谷，浪迹无名的国土——因为我在追寻金鹿。

69

I hunt for the golden stag.

You may smile, my friends, but I pursue the vision that eludes me.

I run across hills and dales, I wander through nameless lands, because I am hunting for the golden stag.

You come and buy in the market and go back to your homes laden with goods, but the spell of the homeless winds has touched me I know not when and where.

I have no care in my heart; all my belongings I have left far behind me.

I run across hills and dales, I wander through nameless lands—because I am hunting for the golden stag.

70

我想起儿时的一天，我在水沟里漂一只纸船。

那是七月的一个雨天，我独自玩得流连忘返。

我在水沟里漂我的纸船。

忽然，阴云密布，狂风大作，暴雨如注。

一条条浑浊的水流溢出水面，淹没了我的纸船。

我心里难过地埋怨：暴风雨故意来破坏我的快乐，所有的恶意都是针对我。

如今，七月的阴天悠长，我在回想人生中那些屡战屡败的时光。

当我抱怨命运的百般捉弄，我忽然想起沉没在水沟里的那只纸船。

70

I remember a day in my childhood I floated a paper boat in the ditch.

It was a wet day of July; I was alone and happy over my play.

I floated my paper boat in the ditch.

Suddenly the storm clouds thickened, winds came in gusts, and rain poured in torrents.

Rills of muddy water rushed and swelled the stream and sunk my boat.

Bitterly I thought in my mind that the storm came on purpose to spoil my happiness; all its malice was against me.

The cloudy day of July is long today, and I have been musing over all those games in life wherein I was loser.

I was blaming my fate for the many tricks it played on me, when suddenly I remembered the paper boat that sank in the ditch.

71

白昼未完，河岸上的集市未散。

我曾担心挥霍了光阴，最终一文不名。

但是，没有，我的兄弟，我还剩下一些东西。命运并没有把我的一切都骗走。

买卖都已完成。

双方货款都已结清，该是我回家的时候。

但是，守门人，你要收通行的费用？

不要担心，我还剩下一些东西。命运并没有把我的一切都骗走。

暂歇的风预示着风暴，西面低垂的云是不祥之兆。

寂静的水流等待着狂风。

我赶在夜幕降临之前过河。

船夫呵，你要收费呀！

是的，兄弟，我还剩下一些东西。命运并没有把我的一切都骗走。

路旁的树下坐着个乞丐。唉，他带着胆怯的希望，抬眼看着我。

他以为我一天的所得，就会变富有。

是的，兄弟，我还剩下一些东西。命运并没有把我的一切都骗走。

夜色渐深，道路寂寞。流萤在叶间闪烁。

是谁在偷偷摸摸地尾随着我？

啊，我知道，是你想抢走我所有的收获。我不会使你失望的！

因为我还剩下一些东西。命运并没有把我的一切都骗走。

我夜半到家，两手空空。

你在门口守候，忧心忡忡，无眠且无言。

你像一只羞怯的小鸟，满怀热爱飞入我的怀抱。

唉，唉，天啊，还剩不少。命运并没有把我的一切都骗走。

71

The day is not yet done, the fair is not over, the fair on the river-bank.

I had feared that my time had been squandered and my last penny lost.

But no, my brother, I have still something left. My fate has not cheated me of everything.

The selling and buying are over.

All the dues on both sides have been gathered in, and it is time for me to go home.

But, gatekeeper, do you ask for your toll?

Do not fear, I have still something left. My fate has not cheated me of everything.

The lull in the wind threatens storm, and the lowering clouds in the west bode no good.

The hushed water waits for the wind.

I hurry to cross the river before the night overtakes me.

O ferryman, you want your fee!

Yes, brother, I have still something left. My fate has not cheated me of everything.

In the wayside under the tree sits the beggar. Alas, he looks at my face with a timid hope!

He thinks I am rich with the day's profit.

Yes, brother, I have still something left. My fate has not cheated me of everything.

The night grows dark and the road lonely. Fireflies gleam among the leaves.

Who are you that follow me with stealthy silent steps?

Ah, I know, it is your desire to rob me of all my gains. I will not disappoint you!

For I still have something left, and my fate has not cheated me of everything.

At midnight I reach home. My hands are empty.

You are waiting with anxious eyes at my door, sleepless and silent.

Like a timorous bird you fly to my breast with eager love.

Ay, ay, my God, much remains still. My fate has not cheated me of everything.

72

经过几天的煎熬，我建起一座寺庙。它没有门，也没有窗，四壁是用巨石砌成的厚厚的墙。

我忘却其他的一切，我躲避大千世界，我全神贯注地凝视着我在祭坛上树立的神像。

里面总是黑夜，被香油的灯照亮。

熏香袅袅，把我的心萦绕。

我彻夜不眠，我用杂乱的线条，在墙上画出荒诞的形象——生翼马、人面花、美女蛇。

没有地方可以传来鸟儿的鸣唱，树叶的呢喃，或是村庄的熙熙攘攘。

只有我的咏唱，在黑暗的穹顶回荡。

我的头脑敏锐而沉静，如火焰的光芒；我的感官陶醉于欣喜若狂。

我不知时光如何消逝，直至雷劈庙毁、痛彻心扉。

灯光显得苍白而羞愧；墙上的画像，宛如被锁住的梦，在灯光下呆呆地凝望，仿佛想要把自己隐藏。

我看着祭坛上的神像。我看见它微笑，它因为神的抚摸而生机盎然。被我囚禁的黑夜展开翅膀，消失不见。

72

With days of hard travail I raised a temple. It had no doors or windows, its walls were thickly built with massive stones.

I forgot all else, I shunned all the world, I gazed in rapt contemplation at the image I had set upon the altar.

It was always night inside, and lit by the lamps of perfumed oil.

The ceaseless smoke of incense wound my heart in its heavy coils.

Sleepless, I carved on the walls fantastic figures in mazy bewildering lines—winged horses, flowers with human faces, women with limbs like serpents.

No passage was left anywhere through which could enter the song of birds, the murmur of leaves, or hum of the busy village.

The only sound that echoed in its dark dome was that of incantations which I chanted.

My mind became keen and still like a pointed flame, my senses swooned in ecstasy.

I knew not how time passed till the thunderstone had struck the temple, and a pain stung me through the heart.

The lamp looked pale and ashamed; the carvings on the walls, like chained dreams, stared meaningless in the light as they would fain hide themselves.

I looked at the image on the altar. I saw it smiling and alive with the living touch of God. The night I had imprisoned had spread its wings and vanished.

73

无限的财富并不属于您，我坚忍而忧郁的大地母亲！

尽管食物短缺，你仍操劳着填满孩子们的嘴。

你给我们的欢乐馈赠，从来就不完美。

你为孩子们做的玩具脆弱易碎。

你无法满足我们的所有渴望，但我就能为此把你抛弃？

你的微笑含着苦悲，在我眼中如此甜美。

你的爱意还不完美，在我心中弥足珍贵。

你用乳汁给我们以生命而非永恒，因此你的眼睛永远清醒。

你长年累月用色彩和歌声来劳动，然而尚未建起天堂，仅有天堂悲伤的迹象。

你创造的美，布满泪水。

我将把我的歌声注入你无声的心里，把我的爱注入你的爱中。

我将以劳动把你赞美。

大地母亲，我见过你慈祥的脸庞，我爱你哀伤的微尘。

73

Infinite wealth is not yours, my patient and dusky mother dust!

You toil to fill the mouths of your children, but food is scarce.

The gift of gladness that you have for us is never perfect.

The toys that you make for your children are fragile.

You cannot satisfy all our hungry hopes, but should I desert you for that?

Your smile which is shadowed with pain is sweet to my eyes.

Your love which knows not fulfi-lment is dear to my heart.

From your breast you have fed us with life but not immortality, that is why your eyes are ever wakeful.

For ages you are working with colour and song, yet your heaven is not built, but only its sad suggestion.

Over your creations of beauty there is the mist of tears.

I will pour my songs into your mute heart, and my love into your love.

I will worship you with labour.

I have seen your tender face and I love your mournful dust, Mother Earth.

74

在大千世界的殿堂，朴素的草叶与阳光、子夜的繁星济济一堂。

我的诗行与云彩和森林的乐章，同样在世界的心中旗鼓相当。

而你，即使富甲一方，你的财富也比不上那单纯的辉煌——太阳喜悦的金黄和月亮沉思的柔光。

天空包罗万象，它的祝福并不落在财富之上。

当死神来临，它便苍白枯萎，零落成尘。

74

In the world's audience hall, the simple blade of grass sits on the same carpet with the sunbeam and the stars of midnight.

Thus my songs share their seats in the heart of the world with the music of the clouds and forests.

But, you man of riches, your wealth has no part in the simple grandeur of the sun's glad gold and the mellow gleam of the musing moon.

The blessing of the all-embracing sky is not shed upon it.

And when death appears, it pales and withers and crumbles into dust.

75

午夜时分，那个想做苦行僧的人宣告：

"现在是离家求神的时候。啊，是谁让我执迷不悟如此之久？"

"是我。"神细语低声。而这个人没有去听。

他的妻子怀里抱着熟睡的婴儿，安静地睡在床的那头。

那人说道："是谁愚弄了我这么久？"

那声音又道："是神。"而他听不到。

婴儿在梦中大叫，依偎着他的母亲。

神命令道："站住，傻瓜，不要离开你的家。"而他还是听不到。

神叹息着抱怨道："为什么我的信徒抛弃我，却又四处把我寻找？"

75

At midnight the would-be ascetic announced:

"This is the time to give up my home and seek for God. Ah, who has held me so long in delusion here?"

God whispered, "I," but the ears of the man were stopped.

With a baby asleep at her breast lay his wife, peacefully sleeping on one side of the bed.

The man said, "Who are ye that have fooled me so long?"

The voice said again, "They are God," but he heard it not.

The baby cried out in its dream, nestling close to its mother.

God commanded, "Stop, fool, leave not thy home," but still he heard not.

God sighed and complained, "Why does my servant wander to seek me, forsaking me?"

76

庙会在庙前举行。雨从早到晚下个不停。

比人群中所有的欢乐都要灿烂的是一个小女孩的灿烂笑容，她只花一分钱便买了一个棕榈叶哨子。

哨子尖锐的欢叫声，飘浮在一切欢笑和喧嚣的上空。

络绎不绝的人群拥来，摩肩接踵。道路泥泞，河水汹涌，田地淹没在无休止的雨中。

比人群中所有的烦恼都要大的是一个小男孩的烦恼——他想买一根彩棒，却一文不名。

他那凝望而惆怅的眼睛，使所有人的庙会如此令人同情。

The fair was on before the temple. It had rained from the early morning and the day came to its end.

Brighter than all the gladness of the crowd was the bright smile of a girl who bought for a farthing a whistle of palm leaf.

The shrill joy of that whistle floated above all laughter and noise.

An endless throng of people came and jostled together. The road was muddy, the river in flood, the field under water in ceaseless rain.

Greater than all the troubles of the crowd was a little boy's trouble—he had not a farthing to buy a painted stick.

His wistful eyes gazing at the shop made this whole meeting of men so pitiful.

西边来的工匠和他的妻子在忙着为砖窑挖土制砖。

他们的小女儿来到河边的渡口；她没完没了地刷洗着盆盆罐罐。

她的小弟弟剃着光头，黝黑裸露的四肢沾满泥浆，跟在她身后，在高高的河岸上，听话地耐心等候。

她头顶着满满的水罐，左手提着闪亮的铜壶，右手拉着小弟弟往家走——她是妈妈的小丫头，繁重的家务让她变得严肃。

有一天我看见这光屁股的小男孩伸腿坐着。

他的姐姐坐在水里，用一把沙土转来转去地擦洗着水壶。

附近有一只毛茸茸的羊羔在岸边吃草。

羊羔走近小男孩身边，突然咩咩地大叫，小男孩吓得跳起来尖叫。

他姐姐放下水壶，跑上岸来。

她一手抱起弟弟，一手抱起羊羔，把她的爱分成两半，人类的小孩和动物的幼崽连接于爱的纽带。

The workman and his wife from the west country are busy digging to make bricks for the kiln.

Their little daughter goes to the landing-place by the river; there she has no end of scouring and scrubbing of pots and pans.

Her little brother, with shaven head and brown, naked, mud-covered limbs, follows after her and waits patiently on the high bank at her bidding.

She goes back home with the full pitcher poised on her head, the shining brass pot in her left hand, holding the child with her right—she the tiny servant of her mother, grave with the weight of the household cares.

One day I saw this naked boy sitting with legs outstretched.

In the water his sister sat rubbing a drinking-pot with a handful of earth, turning it round and round.

Near by a soft-haired lamb stood grazing along the bank.

It came close to where the boy sat and suddenly bleated aloud, and the child started up and screamed.

His sister left off cleaning her pot and ran up.

She took up her brother in one arm and the lamb in the other, and dividing her caresses between them bound in one bond of affection the offspring of beast and man.

78

　　那是在五月天。炎炎的正午仿佛无尽地悠长。干燥的大地在热浪里干渴地打着哈欠。

　　此时，我听到河边传来一声呼喊："亲爱的，来吧！"

　　我合上书，打开窗户向外望去。

　　我看见一只大水牛站在河边，身上污泥斑斑，眼神沉静而耐心；一个小伙子站在没膝的水里，正呼唤它去洗澡。

　　我开怀而笑，心里感到一丝甜蜜。

78

It was in May. The sultry noon seemed endlessly long. The dry earth gaped with thirst in the heat.

When I heard from the riverside a voice calling, "Come, my darling!"

I shut my book and opened the window to look out.

I saw a big buffalo with mud-stained hide standing near the river with placid, patient eyes; and a youth, knee-deep in water, calling it to its bath.

I smiled amused and felt a touch of sweetness in my heart.

79

我常常在想，兽心不懂人的言语，人与兽的界限究竟在哪里隐藏。

在远古的创世之晨，穿越怎样的原始天堂，人与兽的心曾通过简单的小径彼此拜访。

尽管他们的亲缘关系早已被遗忘，他们不断前行的足迹却源远流长。

而模糊的记忆突然苏醒在无言的乐章，兽带着温柔的信任凝视着人的脸庞，人也怀着愉悦的深情把兽的眼睛俯身端详。

仿佛两个朋友戴着面具彼此相望，透过伪装隐约认识了对方。

79

I often wonder where lie hidden the boundaries of recognition between man and the beast whose heart knows no spoken language.

Through what primal paradise in a remote morning of creation ran the simple path by which their hearts visited each other.

Those marks of their constant tread have not been effaced though their kinship has been long forgotten.

Yet suddenly in some wordless music the dim memory wakes up and the beast gazes into the man's face with a tender trust, and the man looks down into its eyes with amused affection.

It seems that the two friends meet masked, and vaguely know each other through the disguise.

佳人，你惊鸿一瞥，便使诗人们所有的诗歌黯然失色！

而你对他们的赞美充耳不闻，因此我来把你赞美。

你让天下最高傲的人在你脚下自惭形秽。

而你对那些默默无闻的人们满怀热爱，因此我把你崇拜。

你的手臂堪称完美，她们的触碰将为帝王的尊贵增添光辉。

而你却用她们来扫除灰尘，使陋室生辉，因此我对你充满敬畏。

80

With a glance of your eyes you could plunder all the wealth of songs struck from poets' harps, fair woman!

But for their praises you have no ear, therefore I come to praise you.

You could humble at your feet the proudest heads in the world.

But it is your loved ones, unknown to fame, whom you choose to worship, therefore I worship you.

The perfection of your arms would add glory to kingly splendour with their touch.

But you use them to sweep away the dust, and to make clean your humble home, therefore I am filled with awe.

81

死神呵，我的死神，你为何在我耳畔细语轻声？

当夜幕降临，花儿凋零，牛儿归棚，你悄悄地来到我的身边，说着我不懂的语言。

死神呵，我的死神，难道你必须用昏沉的呢喃和冷酷的亲吻，来向我求爱并赢得我的芳心？

难道我们的婚礼不会盛大铺张？

难道你不系一个花环在褐色的鬈发上？

死神呵，我的死神，难道没有人在你面前让旗帜飘扬，难道黑夜不会因你的红色火炬而光芒万丈？

来吧，不眠之夜，海螺声声。

给我穿上红艳的披风，抓住我的手，携手同行。

且让马车在门口等候，任由马儿不住地嘶鸣。

死神呵，我的死神，且掀起我的面纱，自豪地端详我的脸庞。

81

Why do you whisper so faintly in my ears, O Death, my Death?

When the flowers droop in the evening and cattle come back to their stalls, you stealthily come to my side and speak words that I do not understand.

Is this how you must woo and win me with the opiate of drowsy murmur and cold kisses, O Death, my Death?

Will there be no proud ceremony for our wedding?

Will you not tie up with a wreath your tawny coiled locks?

Is there none to carry your banner before you, and will not the night be on fire with your red torch-lights, O Death, my Death?

Come with your conch-shells sounding, come in the sleepless night.

Dress me with a crimson mantle, grasp my hand and take me.

Let your chariot be ready at my door with your horses neighing impatiently.

Raise my veil and look at my face proudly, O Death, my Death!

82

今夜，我和我的新娘要玩死亡的游戏。

夜色漆黑，空中风云变幻，海上波涛怒吼。

我和我的新娘，离开梦的温床，推门出去。

我们坐在秋千上，狂风在背后猛烈地推着我们。

我的新娘开始又惊又喜，颤抖着依偎在我的胸口。

我温柔地安抚她许久。

我为她布下繁花满床，我关上房门，把光拒之门外。

我轻吻她的双唇，在她耳畔细语呢喃，直至她慵懒地半梦半醒。

她沉醉在无尽的朦胧甜蜜之中。

她对我的爱抚没有回应，我的歌声也没能把她唤醒。

今夜风暴的呼唤，从旷野传到我们的耳畔。

我的新娘颤抖着站起，她抓住我的手走出去。

她的头发在风中飞舞，她的面纱飘扬，她的花环在胸前簌簌作响。

死亡的推动使她重获新生。

我和我的新娘，面对面，心连心。

82

We are to play the game of death to-night, my bride and I.

The night is black, the clouds in the sky are capricious, and the waves are raving at sea.

We have left our bed of dreams, flung open the door and come out, my bride and I.

We sit upon a swing, and the storm winds give us a wild push from behind.

My bride starts up with fear and delight, she trembles and clings to my breast.

Long have I served her tenderly.

I made for her a bed of flowers and I closed the doors to shut out the rude light from her eyes.

I kissed her gently on her lips and whispered softly in her ears till she half swooned in languor.

She was lost in the endless mist of vague sweetness.

She answered not to my touch, my songs failed to arouse

her.

To-night has come to us the call of the storm from the wild.

My bride has shivered and stood up, she has clasped my hand and come out.

Her hair is flying in the wind, her veil is fluttering, her garland rustles over her breast.

The push of death has swung her into life.

We are face to face and heart to heart, my bride and I.

83

　　她住在玉米田边的山坡上，附近泉水叮咚，流过古树庄严的倒影。女人们来这里装满她们的水罐，旅人们会坐在这里休息谈天。她每天劳动和做梦，伴随着溪流潺潺。

　　一天傍晚，陌生人从云雾缭绕的山峰下来，他的头发像困倦的蛇一样纷乱。我们惊奇地问："你是谁呀？"他没有回答，只坐在潺潺的水边，默默地注视着她住的茅屋。我们的心吓得乱颤，我们回到家时天色已晚。

　　次日清晨，汲水的女人们来到雪松旁的泉边，她们发现她的茅屋门户洞开，而人声杳然，哪里有她的笑脸？地上躺着空罐，墙角的油灯早已烧完。没有人知道天亮之前她逃去了哪里——陌生人也已不见。

　　五月天，阳光日渐强烈，冰雪消散，我们哭泣着坐在泉边。我们心中想念："她去的地方是否有山泉？炎热干渴的日子里，她到哪里去装满她的水罐？"我们沮丧地彼此询问："可有地方在我们住的山外面？"

　　那是一个夏日的夜晚，微风从南方吹来；我坐在她的空屋里，残灯依旧，仍未点燃。突然，群山在我眼前消失不见，仿佛拉开的窗帘。"啊，是她来了。我的孩子，别来无恙？你是否开心？而在这露天之下，你在何处栖身？唉，可惜我们的泉水不能缓解你的干渴。"

"那里是同一片天空，"她说，"只是不受群山的阻隔——同一条溪流，汇聚成江河；——同一片土地，扩展成平川。""一应俱全，"我叹道，"只是我们不在。"她的笑里带着遗憾："你们在我心中。"我在夜色中醒来，听着溪流叮咚，萧萧雪松，声如涛涌。

83

She dwelt on the hillside by the edge of a maize-field, near the spring that flows in laughing rills through the solemn shadows of ancient trees. The women came there to fill their jars, and travellers would sit there to rest and talk. She worked and dreamed daily to the tune of the bubbling stream.

One evening the stranger came down from the cloud-hidden peak; his locks were tangled like drowsy snakes. We asked in wonder, "Who are you?" He answered not but sat by the garrulous stream and silently gazed at the hut where she dwelt. Our hearts quaked in fear and we came back home when it was night.

Next morning when the women came to fetch water at the spring by the *deodar* trees, they found the doors open in her hut, but her voice was gone and where was her smiling face? The empty jar lay on the floor and her lamp had burnt itself out in the corner. No one knew where she had fled to before it was morning—and the stranger had gone.

In the month of May the sun grew strong and the snow melted, and we sat by the spring and wept. We wondered in our mind, "Is there a spring in the land where she has gone and where she can fill her vessel in these hot thirsty days?" And we asked each other in dismay, "Is there a land beyond these hills where we live?"

It was a summer night; the breeze blew from the south; and I sat in her deserted room where the lamp stood still unlit. When suddenly from before my eyes the hills vanished like curtains drawn aside. "Ah, it is she who comes. How are you, my child? Are you happy? But where can you shelter under this open sky? And, alas! our spring is not here to allay your thirst."

"Here is the same sky," she said, "only free from the fencing hills, —this is the same stream grown into a river,— the same earth widened into a plain." "Everything is here," I sighed, "only we are not." She smiled sadly and said, "You are in my heart." I woke up and heard the babbling of the stream and the rustling of the *deodars* at night.

84

秋云被疾驰的太阳追赶，影子略过黄绿相间的稻田。

蜜蜂在阳光里沉醉，忘记了啜饮蜂蜜，傻傻地哼唱盘旋。

鸭群在河中的小岛，无缘无故地欢叫。

兄弟们，今天早晨，谁也不要回家，谁也不要去上班。

让我们乘着风暴占领蓝天，飞奔着抢夺空间。

欢笑声在空中飘荡，仿佛泡沫漂在洪流之上。

兄弟们，且让我们在徒劳的歌声中挥霍我们的早晨。

84

Over the green and yellow rice-fields sweep the shadows of the autumn clouds followed by the swift-chasing sun.

The bees forget to sip their honey; drunken with light they foolishly hover and hum.

The ducks in the islands of the river clamour in joy for mere nothing.

Let none go back home, brothers, this morning, let none go to work.

Let us take the blue sky by storm and plunder space as we run.

Laughter floats in the air like foam on the flood.

Brothers, let us squander our morning in futile songs.

85

　　读者呵，你是谁，百年之后在我的诗里徜徉？

　　我不能从春天的宝藏里送你一朵鲜花，从天边的云彩里送你一缕金霞。

　　打开门来眺望吧。

　　从你繁花盛开的花园里，采撷百年前消逝之花记忆的的芬芳。

　　在你心中的欢乐里，愿你感受到鲜活的喜悦，曾在一个春天的清晨欢唱，将它欢快的歌声穿越百年的时光。

85

Who are you, reader, reading my poems an hundred years hence?

I cannot send you one single flower from this wealth of the spring, one single streak of gold from yonder clouds.

Open your doors and look abroad.

From your blossoming garden gather fragrant memories of the vanished flowers of an hundred years before.

In the joy of your heart may you feel the living joy that sang one spring morning, sending its glad voice across an hundred years.